In addition to pinning down the essential characteristics of these major approaches to analysis, this study details their strengths and weaknesses and offers an important set of guidelines for their application to concrete research activities.

ABOUT THE AUTHOR

ORAN R. YOUNG, Ph.D., is an assistant professor in the Department of Politics, and a faculty associate of the Center of International Studies at Princeton University. The author of *The Intermediaries: Third Parties in International Crises* and numerous articles in such publications as the *General Systems Yearbook*, the *China Quarterly*, and the *Bulletin of the Atomic Scientists*, Dr. Young also serves as associate editor of *World Politics*.

FOUNDATIONS OF MODERN POLITICAL SCIENCE SERIES
Robert A. Dahl, Editor

SYSTEMS OF POLITICAL SCIENCE

Systems

of Political

Science

FOUNDATIONS OF MODERN POLITICAL SCIENCE SERIES

O R A N   R .   Y O U N G

Princeton University

ENGLEWOOD CLIFFS, NEW JERSEY · Prentice-Hall, Inc.

Current printing (last digit):

12 11 10 9 8 7 6 5 4 3 2 1

FOUNDATIONS OF MODERN POLITICAL SCIENCE SERIES

Robert A. Dahl, Editor

To Marit

Preface

This volume constitutes an attempt to formulate a new
conception of approaches to political analysis. This conception
focuses squarely on a number of the presently ambiguous problems
concerning the scope of the discipline rather than on various currently
popular but intrinsically somewhat narrow considerations dealing with
means or techniques for the manipulation of data. At the same time,
the conception presented in this volume directs itself toward
carving out a solid middle ground for approaches to analysis between
full-fledged theories on the one hand and simple perspectives or points
of view on the other hand. This posture clearly involves clipping
the wings of some of the more far-reaching hopes for approaches
to analysis and assuming a rather modest view of the functions
of the various approaches. It turns out, nevertheless, that the relevant

middle ground is substantial and that the functions to which these approaches can address themselves are of great importance.

The present work is certainly not inclusive in the sense of dealing with all of the current approaches to political analysis, although it does treat a number of the most outstanding and influential of the reigning approaches. Its most fundamental concern, however, is to pin down the essential characteristics of systematic approaches to political analysis. It therefore passes over various approaches as, for example, organization theory, the theory of bargaining and the political man approach in order to facilitate a more extensive discussion of several other particularly influential approaches. Even so, the substantive chapters of this book are directed more toward an effort to catch the essence of various approaches than toward an attempt to perform an exhaustive analysis of any one of them. This in itself is not, however, an easy task. Insofar as an approach to analysis is not a full-fledged or formal theory, part of the influence or popularity that it attains stems from its peculiar qualities of concept formation and linguistic imaginativeness. For this reason, approaches to analysis are invariably difficult to summarize. Though I have attempted to perform this task as fairly and fluently as possible, I have no doubt that my efforts along these lines will provide material for many critics.

I wish to acknowledge my gratitude for assistance from several sources. Above all, I would like to thank Karl Deutsch for stimulating my interest in this general area some years ago as well as for assisting me to arrange for the present enterprise. Robert Dahl was instrumental both in introducing me to the Foundations of Modern Political Science series and in offering me valuable advice on a variety of subjects which I have generally tried to keep in mind in putting this study together. Beyond this, I should also extend my thanks to Marion Levy not only for offering assistance with the various intricacies of structural functionalism but especially for playing the role of constructive gadfly and inducing me to rethink a number of key issues involved in this study. Finally, my thanks go to the Center of International Studies at Princeton University for its role in creating a supportive atmosphere in which to work on this study as well as for assistance of a more material sort.

Princeton, N.J.   *Oran R. Young*
1967

Preface

Contents

xii

Contents

Contents

Politics and the Nature of Approaches to Analysis

The Scope of Political Science

There is little consensus among political
scientists on the general scope and boundaries
of their discipline. In fact, a perusal of the literature
leads quickly to a proliferation of divergent
propositions concerning this question. The best that can be done
is to group the various views into several broad categories,
a number of which stand out rather clearly.

Many writers, and especially those whose views can be classified as essentially traditional, approach political analysis from an institutional perspective. Their emphasis is generally on the state and its sub-units as governing structures. Rodee, Anderson, and Christol, for example, suggest that " 'Political science' may be defined as 'the science of the state,' or as 'a branch of the social sciences dealing with the theory, organization, government, and practice of the state.' "[1] Those who belong in this category sometimes also insist that the institutions under analysis must be legal or legally founded, but this addition is by no means universal.

Related to these perspectives is a second general orientation that focuses on the governance of territory and on the notion of governmental functions. Typical of this viewpoint is the position of Max Weber, that an organization or association can be considered political "if and insofar as the enforcement of its order is carried out continually within a given territorial area by the application and threat of physical force on the part of the administrative staff."[2] Here too, various institutions tend to become the primary units of analysis. But now the scope of political science is delineated in terms of the establishment and maintenance of order over geographical areas.

These viewpoints on the proper scope of political science stem from the early years of this century and have long been solidly entrenched. Surveys of political studies completed in the early decades of the twentieth century demonstrate the predominance of these perspectives. Focus on institutions, the state, and the governance of territory did not, however, preclude the proliferation of new propositions concerning the scope of political science.

Perhaps the first new orientation to become widely influential was the view that political science should concern itself with the nature, locus, and utilization of power. The focus of interest shifts in this approach from institutions themselves to the accumulation and exercise of *power* wherever it is found. In this context, the unit of analysis is not necessarily the institution at various levels of formal organization. The relations of power are analyzed as they become manifest in a great variety of situations. As Robson puts it, "The 'focus of interest' of the political scientist is clear and unambiguous; it centers on the struggle to gain or retain power, to exercise power or influence over others, or to resist that exercise."[3]

A further development which can be traced back to the 1930's but

---

[1] C. C. Rodee, T. J. Anderson, and C. Q. Christol, *Introduction to Political Science* (New York: McGraw-Hill, 1957), p. 4.

[2] Max Weber, as cited in Robert A. Dahl, *Modern Political Analysis* (Englewood Cliffs, N.J.: Prentice-Hall, 1963), p. 5.

[3] William A. Robson, *The University Teaching of Social Sciences: Political Science* (Paris: UNESCO, 1954), pp. 17–18.

Politics and the Nature of Approaches to Analysis

which has enjoyed widespread acceptance only in more recent years outlines the scope of political science in terms of the relations and patterns of interaction among individuals. The central shift involved here is the focusing on the individual as the primary unit of political analysis. Politics becomes "an aspect of human behavior in an environment."[4] And some of the purposes or goals of human beings together with many of the methods for their attainment are taken to be political. The specific criteria for making the distinction between political and nonpolitical goals and methods vary from analyst to analyst.

Even more recently, several new viewpoints on the scope of political science have begun to emerge. These bear a relationship to each other because they all deal ultimately with the production and allocation of *values* in a society. There are, however, at least three interesting variations on this general theme in the current literature. A first viewpoint focuses on the making and execution of decisions. The decision, which may be conceived of as a selection among several programmatic alternatives for the allocation of values, becomes the unit of analysis. Further factors such as the authoritativeness and the effectiveness of decisions as well as the probability of their enforcement are typically added to the basic focus on decisions in this perspective.

A related orientation conceptualizes the scope of political science in terms of policies and policy-making. Ranney maintains that "Taken together . . . political science has dealt with both policy content and policy process, and has considered each of them both descriptively and evaluatively."[5] Policies are generally seen as instrumental programs for the attainment of stated goals, and analysis along these lines typically deals with the processes of making, grouping, and altering policies at various levels in the over-all social system. Closely related to the policy perspective is the orientation which defines the political function "as that of facilitating the effective attainment of a collectivity's goals."[6] The principal difference here is that this last viewpoint focuses more on questions concerning goals and teleology than on the precise nature of instrumental processes.

A first glance at the proliferation of viewpoints concerning the scope of political science presents a picture of some real disagreement and even confusion in the discipline. There are, however, several factors that mitigate this initial impression at least to some extent. Above all, there are strong indications that disagreements concerning the scope of political

[4] Vernon Van Dyke, *Political Science: A Philosophical Analysis* (Stanford: Stanford University Press, 1960), p. 3.

[5] Austin Ranney, *The Governing of Man* (New York: Holt, 1958), p. 582.

[6] Talcott Parsons, "An Outline of the Social System," in Talcott Parsons, Edward Shils, Kaspar Naegele, and Jesse Pitts (eds.), *Theories of Society* (New York: The Free Press of Glencoe, 1961), p. 52.

Politics and the Nature of Approaches to Analysis

science are much more extensive and radical at the level of abstract and epistemological analyses of the scope of the discipline than at the more concrete level of substantive research. The point is simply that substantive political analyses can generally be recognized as belonging in the field of political science without great difficulty. After divergent chapters concerning theoretical frameworks and conceptualizations, many political analyses begin to show increasing signs of belonging in the same general field of study. Perhaps the most substantial ambiguities in this context presently stem from the upswing of interdisciplinary work leading to an integration of some aspects of political science with sociology and psychology. But ambiguities of this variety are increasing in many disciplines at this point in time.

The fissures that appear in the discussion of a wide range of standpoints concerning the scope of political science also seem to obscure one basic and underlying divergence which divides the various perspectives. This divergence separates a "broad" and a "narrow" view of politics and political phenomena. The broad view focuses on political *functions* and treats politics as a process or type of activity. Those who adhere to this view tend to be interested in most aspects of social systems and to find political phenomena almost everywhere. With this orientation, for example, it is possible to speak of the politics of the family, the corporation, the association, the church, and so forth; there is no hesitation in treating as politics a variety of activities that may constitute only a part-time consideration for a given actor and that may even be far from that actor's main concern in operating in its own arena. The narrow view, on the other hand, tends to emphasize political *structures* and to orient itself toward various types of political institutions. Adherents of this view tend to range much less widely over the various aspects of social systems focusing their attention, for the most part, on structures that deal with politics on a full-time basis and that are explicitly labeled as pertaining to the political or governmental subsystem of the society.

From this vantage point it becomes clear that the standpoints centering on political institutions and the governance of territory subscribe basically to a narrow view while standpoints focusing on such phenomena as policies and decisions are almost inevitably more compatible with a broad view. And the stirrings in the 1930's that led to the generation of the power perspective and the emphasis on the individual as a unit of analysis can be seen as part of an early trend breaking away from the narrow view which had previously been dominant in political science. In a rough sense, then, this dichotomy not only divides the various views on the scope of political science, but it also tends to point up an important current trend in the discipline. Although the narrow view has not been discarded, there has

4

been a rather strong movement toward broader views of politics as time has passed; this trend is undoubtedly related to the general impression of fractionation which cannot be avoided in surveying the discipline of political science today.

It is pointless to attempt to bring order in this field by choosing among the perspectives on scope outlined above or by elaborating a new or synthetic view. Each of the orientations in question has something to offer and, above all, their very nature is such that any choice among them would involve some subjective decisions and value judgments. It is possible, however, to outline and classify the principal variables, factors, concepts, and questions that political scientists generally deal with in their analyses. In this way we can construct a useful overview of the subject matter of political science.

Probably the most basic set of variables and organizing concepts in any discipline can be labeled descriptive. The subject matter of much work in political science falls into this category of description, whose effort is more to delineate relevant phenomena, to generate useful classifications and breakdowns, and to pinpoint the important characteristics of political activities than to explain complex patterns of events, to extrapolate and evaluate trends, or to make predictions.

Although descriptive analyses have generally been heavily criticized in recent years, there are several points that may appropriately be made in defense of description. To start with, descriptive work tends to stand in a logically antecedent relationship to other more sophisticated and penetrating techniques of analysis. And there are many areas of political science in which the descriptive foundation is still so weak that it is virtually imperative to begin with descriptive analyses. In addition, rigorous, systematic description is a notably successful method of generating useful insights and hypotheses. A related point follows from the theory of categorization, which states that two entities or objects that resemble each other in some ways are likely to resemble each other in other ways as well. Systematic description is perhaps the best available technique for elaborating such resemblances and reaping the fruits of the theory of categorization. Finally, systematic description is an important device for the improvement of information retrieval and recall capabilities.

Political analyses frequently deal both with horizontal classifications of political structures and systems and with vertical classifications of levels and hierarchies of political phenomena. Horizontal variables range widely through typologies of governmental systems, economies, bureaucracies, and so forth, while vertical classification tends to focus on system levels and scale effects.

Further descriptive variables and concepts deal with the distinction   **5** between a political entity or system and its environment and with the interaction patterns between the entity and whatever is outside it. Questions in this context concern boundaries, membership, criteria of inclusion and exclusion, isolation, patterns of interaction with other entities, and the notions of inputs and outputs. Then descriptive variables turn to concepts and questions concerning internal or intrasystem patterns. Typical variables here deal with matters such as structures, processes, levels of integration, interdependence of components, structural and functional differentiation, and centralization and decentralization.

A second set of variables and concepts deals with questions that may be grouped under the general heading of pattern maintenance. The principal questions in this instance concern conditions for the maintenance of a basic pattern by a political structure or system and the processes through which such maintenance is achieved. The over-all notion of pattern maintenance does not refer to a static situation but to a set of conditions and mechanisms through which the essential characteristics of a political pattern are kept within the bounds of recognizability.

There are several groups of variables and concepts that fall under this general rubric and that crop up frequently in political analyses. Centrally located are the concepts of stability and equilibrium together with their various ramifications. Then there is a series of concepts dealing with patterns and types of political conflict and with various modes of conflict resolution. Rounding out this set of concepts are questions concerning such variables as legitimacy, authority, and validation.

The whole problem of *patterns of control* makes up the next analytic division of the subject matter of political science. This is an area that has received a great deal of attention in recent political analyses. It does not cover directly problems concerning the production and allocation of values in a society but rather it centers on the analysis of who decides questions concerning such problems and by what means and techniques. Perhaps the touchstone of this category is the problem of political power in its broader senses. In fact, the power-oriented theories and systems of analysis tend to address themselves directly to this part of the general subject matter of political science.

A variety of concepts centering on the questions of power and influence form the core of this category. In this context, the notions of scope, domain, weight, and coerciveness of power and influence are important as are such dichotomies as negative vs. positive coercion and current vs. potential influence. Beyond the immediate concept of power itself, other concepts in this category focus on political resources, strategies and tactics for their utilization, and the influence of skill in shaping patterns of

6

control; these considerations lead inevitably to the analysis of political elites and arenas of political interaction.

A further segment of the subject matter of political science deals with problems of goals, purposes, and goal attainment. As mentioned earlier, some writers go so far as to consider political science the study of that subsystem of the over-all social system concerned with the attainment of societal goals. And although it is not necessary to rely so heavily on a single focus of this kind, it is clear that the effort to achieve objectives and goals as well as the instrumentalities utilized for these purposes forms a part of the subject matter of political science. The minimal goal of survival tends to throw the discussion back to the questions and concepts of pattern maintenance. But political goals are never limited solely to survival, and this broadening of perspectives on goals and values generates new concepts and questions.

In addition to concepts concerning goals, priorities among goals, and opportunity costs, this general category covers many of the variables dealing with policies and policy making. Specifically, questions focus on matters like policy alternatives, consequences of various actions, priorities, probabilities of various outcomes occurring, and attitudes toward uncertainty. These questions are carried further by the distinction between objective possibilities and perceptions in the area of policy making. In short, all the phenomena surrounding the production of values come in for analysis in this context. Finally, this category encompasses some, but not all, of the questions that center on the concept of political functions.

A final division of the subject matter of political science falls under the general heading of patterns of change. Political phenomena rarely if ever remain in static relationships; accordingly, questions have been raised and concepts developed dealing with the subject of political change. In fact a good deal of attention has been devoted to developments and transitions in the nature of political structures and systems. There is, however, another side to the category of political change: political structures and systems do not always move from an old to a new form; they may break down or become disrupted without any corresponding process of transition to new forms. In general, much less attention has been devoted to these problems by political analysts. Nevertheless, important problems do arise in this area that will probably receive more serious thought and analysis in the future.

On the nondisruptive side of this category, questions center around such concepts as evolution, transition, expansion, growth, and especially, modernization. In addition, questions concerning goal-changing processes and the phenomenon of system transformation are important. The problems of breakdown have generated a variety of concepts dealing with such

Politics and the Nature of Approaches to Analysis

matters as revolution, crises, stresses and strains, disruption, decay, decline, and dissolution.

This discussion of the subject matter of political science is by no means exhaustive. It is designed to provide an overview of the discipline and to suggest a way of looking at the work being done in political science that avoids some of the general confusion surrounding the question of the scope of the discipline. As such, this way of looking at the subject matter of political science will be of assistance to the reader in subsequent chapters of this book. Various approaches to analysis will be discussed and compared in terms of the subject areas to which they are primarily relevant.

Approaches to Analysis

This book is primarily a study of various approaches to the analysis of political phenomena. There is a considerable amount of disagreement concerning the essential nature of an approach to analysis, and this has frequently led to serious confusion. It is therefore necessary to discuss the nature of approaches before embarking on an analysis and comparison of the various approaches themselves. There exists a considerable variety of distinguishable views in this area, and a good deal of light can be shed on the problem by taking a brief look at the most important focal points in the debate.

A restrictive view of the nature of an approach emerges from the writings of Robert Merton,[7] who speaks in terms of *general orientations* when dealing with the problem of approaches, and distinguishes them from true *theories*. A general orientation outlines the types of variables that an analysis should take into account, and provides concepts with which to view a particular subject area. In this context the emphasis is on systems of classification, which can become coding schemes for data, rather than on relations among variables or formal hypotheses. In Merton's view the utilization of a general orientation can facilitate the process of arriving at hypotheses but the orientation itself does not encompass the hypotheses. A general orientation can therefore be viewed as a framework for inquiry and as a source of criteria of relevance and importance in selecting data. It should also locate the subject matter under analysis in the broader spectrum of human concerns. And finally, it should provide a general perspective from which to view a subject area or a way of cutting into the mass of data to be analyzed.

A middle position on the nature of approaches is illustrated by recent

[7] Robert Merton, *Social Theory and Social Structure* (Glencoe, Ill.: The Free Press, 1957), pp. 9, 88–92.

Politics and the Nature of Approaches to Analysis

statements of Gabriel Almond.[8] This view parallels Merton's on the matters of variables, concepts, and classifications. But with Almond an approach is considered more than a set of integrated concepts and classificatory schemes, although it is still less than a full-fledged theory. In this view statements concerning relations among concepts and ranges of concepts are integral parts of the approach itself. Such statements stem partly from deductive analysis and partly from the general knowledge of the subject area that the analyst brings to his work. These statements are treated as hypotheses to be subjected to empirical testing when the approach is actually utilized. Nevertheless, such an approach is less than a full-fledged theory because the worth of the suggested categories and hypotheses remains in question until empirical analysis has been done. Questions concerning empirical consistency and validation become relevant at this point.

A third position in this discussion views approaches as essentially deductive theories. Here David Easton's discussion of *conceptual frameworks* becomes relevant.[9] His position overlaps with the others on such matters as concepts, criteria of relevance, and systems of classification, but it goes considerably further to include essentially analytic theory based on deductive reasoning. Easton suggests that a conceptual framework should encompass a series of integrated and consistent propositions deductively derived from the basic postulates and concepts of the approach. In this view, the derived propositions must be capable of subsequent empirical testing and must therefore have definable empirical referents. Utilization of such a conceptual framework consists in testing propositions from the analytic theory against empirical data and making any indicated alterations, modifications, and refinements.

These views on the nature of approaches fall roughly along a spectrum in terms of such variables as the extent of deductive reasoning involved and the formality of statement employed. There are, however, several additional functions which analysts sometimes attribute to approaches. The views of Snyder, Bruck, and Sapin concerning *frames of reference* illustrate some of these functions.[10]

In terms of the considerations outlined above, this posture falls somewhere between those of Merton and Almond. Like Merton, it treats an approach as an *ordering enterprise* focusing on definition, classification, and categorization. But it goes somewhat further in suggesting that the resultant concepts and classifications "can be used as the basis for generat-

[8] Gabriel Almond, "A Developmental Approach to Political Systems," *World Politics,* Vol. XVII, No. 2 (January 1965), pp. 183–214.
[9] David Easton, *The Political System* (New York: Knopf, 1953), pp. 53–59.
[10] R. Snyder, W. Bruck, and B. Sapin (eds.), *Foreign Policy Decision Making* (Glencoe, Ill.: The Free Press, 1963), pp. 26–33.

ing hypotheses" to be tested empirically. In any case, Snyder, Bruck, and Sapin then proceed to outline additional functions that an approach should perform. A complete frame of reference should make explicit the values and norms of those who employ it and provide an "explicit revelation of the observer's general posture toward his subject"[11] as well as indicate his principal assumptions. Finally, a frame of reference should deal with the problem of establishing empirical indices to be employed in its application to specific subject areas. This position concerning the nature of an approach hence goes considerably beyond the factors underlying the spectrum along which the first three positions were placed.

Although the specifications of particular approaches differ markedly, some type of approach is present in all systematic analysis. The approach may be rudimentary in form and it may be tacitly elaborated rather than explicit, but the psychological necessity of utilizing an approach cannot be escaped. The intellectual functions that an approach performs are sufficiently central and extensive to speak meaningfully of the necessity of an approach. These functions can be divided into several major categories.

Above all, an approach deals with some of the central problems of perception. It is generally agreed that the individual is faced with ar overwhelming quantity of potential perceptual cues and that, in fact, h absorbs only a small percentage of these cues. Many cues are screened ou unconsciously while others are accepted or rejected on the basis of conscious criteria of selection. The resultant pattern of reception is partly shaped by psychological socialization and various processes of training and partly developed through the conscious establishment of criteria of relevance and importance. These developmental processes also tend to interact with each other over time. In this context, an approach to analysis can be seen as a rather systematic and consciously developed set of criteria and procedures to help with the problems of perception. Since the potential information in any area of interest cannot be handled in its entirety, an approach is utilized to guide the process of selection.

A second range of functions performed by approaches to analysis centers on the problems of intellectual organization. Even after the initial screening process at the level of perception, the remaining cues are still too bulky and disorganized to be utilized successfully by the human mental apparatus. With nothing more than an initial receptor grid, the human being will still tend to be overwhelmed by great numbers of seemingly disparate cues and consequently to become paralyzed in terms of performing analytic operations in a given subject area. The need here is to bring some order to the available perceptual cues.

In this context, an approach to analysis functions to provide a series of

11 *Ibid.*, p. 29.

Politics and the Nature of Approaches to Analysis

conceptual hierarchies and classificatory frameworks for incoming cues. More specifically, an approach: (1) establishes boundaries so that cues for one subject area can be separated from those for another, (2) lays out important variables which become focal points around which cues can be sorted and clustered, (3) refines rankings of importance leading to a process of placing some cues in a central position while weeding out or downgrading others, and in some cases, (4) supplies hypotheses linking groups of cues and relating them to each other.

These groups of functions are sufficient to justify the proposition concerning the necessity of an approach, but there is one additional group of functions that should perhaps be mentioned at this point. These functions deal with the problems of interpersonal communication, which is based at least on a minimal standardization of word meanings, concepts, categories, and patterns of explanation. In short, communication is impossible unless the meanings attributed to the symbolic systems employed by the participants overlap to some minimal and empirically meaningful extent. In this sense it is possible to consider approaches to analysis as continuations or extensions of linguistic development that become necessary in efforts to communicate beyond a first and simple order of meaning. In order to deal with complex social phenomena or to progress beyond simple descriptive statements to the realm of explanations, predictions, and so forth, one must utilize a level of analysis beyond that characteristic of ordinary language. And this is the point at which systematic approaches to analysis become functionally significant in the processes of communication.

The necessity of approaches to analysis has been demonstrated and their organizational functions have been set forth. This is not to say, however, that there are no problems with approaches. At this point, we should point out some of the pitfalls that should be watched for in utilizing approaches even though the necessity of approaches is accepted. Above all, it is worth noting that an approach to analysis, by its very nature, cannot be wholly objective. An approach may or may not have built-in norms and values of an explicit variety, but it clearly must provide criteria of relevance, importance, and selection in order to deal with data; this implies that it sets up standards that determine inclusion or exclusion of particular data and that further determine the relative importance to be attached to included data. Related to this problem is the fact that the very existence of criteria of selection, conceptual frameworks, and systems of classification inevitably exerts an influence toward prejudging and shaping the outcomes of analysis. Here it is meaningful to distinguish between negative and positive prejudgment. The utilization of a particular approach does not necessarily determine particular conclusions that will be reached in a positive sense. But it will exercise a considerable influence in the more negative sense of canceling out the possibility of reaching a great many logically conceivable outcomes and conclusions.

Another common problem of approaches to analysis is their incompleteness and lack of balance. There is no definitive logical reason why approaches cannot deal with the whole range of questions that are of interest in a field such as political science. On the one hand, however, an approach that did perform this feat would be so extensive and bulky as to become unusable. And on the other hand, it is an empirical fact that approaches to political analysis seldom cover the whole range of possible questions. Then too, the proliferation of approaches in recent years has begun to create new communications problems among analysts. Followers of the same approach gain an added facility in communicating with each other, but communication across the lines of approaches is increasingly hampered by the development of specialized terminology and concepts, the spread of jargon, the divergence of perspectives, and the resultant confusion of meaning. One by-product of this development that may cause increasing problems is its tendency to set in motion a positive feedback process leading to greater inbreeding as opposed to cross-fertilization. Finally, the fact that considerable time and energy is expended in defending approaches against all comers rather than in applying them to substantive analyses must be reckoned as a problem that is commonly generated by the development and utilization of systematic approaches to analysis. Typically the creators of an approach begin to identify very strongly with it and as a result, criticisms of the approach are frequently interpreted as personal attacks; then the recipients of such criticism often feel obliged to take up the cudgels in defense of their own approach. The result is often a series of polemical or semipolemical exchanges.

Conclusion

In recent years the field of political science has been characterized by the development of a variety of alternative approaches to analysis. A number of these approaches associated with the development of a systematic and empirical political science receive analytic treatment in the substantive chapters of this book. In this work no attempt will be made to establish the position of any specific approach over the others under discussion. Such is not the function of this volume. Rather, an effort will be made to pin down the various approaches in terms of boundary conditions and content and to make some rough comparisons among them on the basis of several indicators. In addition, the following material will deal with the utility of these approaches in analyzing the segments of the subject matter of political science and with characteristic problems which each of them generates.

12

Politics and the Nature of Approaches to Analysis

General
Systems
Theory
and Political
Analysis

In recent years a number of systemic approaches
to political analysis have become quite prominent in the literature.
These approaches stem, at least conceptually, from general
systems theory. This body of theory has only recently begun
to attract serious attention from political scientists, although haphazard
and confused references have been made to it from time
to time. General systems theory itself,
nevertheless, has a good deal to offer political scientists interested
in approaches to analysis. This chapter therefore focuses

on general systems theory proper, while the next chapter deals with several of the more familiar systemic approaches that are ultimately derivatives of general systems theory in an analytic, if not an historical, sense.

The Nature of General Systems Theory

Some years ago a number of analysts, especially in several of the natural sciences, began to feel more and more strongly that important opportunities for advances in research were being lost because of several practices that were, and still are to a large extent, prevalent at the time. Above all, they protested against the tendency toward rigid compartmentalization of disciplines and the consequent reduction of cross flows between various fields of research leading to duplication of efforts. Such practices tend both to impede progress in each specific field and to result in inefficiencies since basic theoretical and conceptual advances often have to be made over and over again as one field after another becomes interested in analogous problems. At the same time, the group felt that the tendency of many disciplines to concern themselves with specific phenomena and detailed studies to the exclusion of abstract and general theoretical considerations was leading to an inability to integrate meaningfully the knowledge acquired in other disciplines. From this perspective, they emphasized the great importance for any discipline of having a solid foundation in general and abstract theory and the consequent importance of allocating some research time and resources to studies at fairly high levels of abstraction. These points were linked to the scientific method in terms of the important functions of broad conceptual guidelines and general perspectives on ways of cutting into bodies of data as prerequisites for successful analysis at more detailed levels. In short, general systems theory originated in a movement aimed at the unification of science and scientific analysis.[1]

The origins of general systems theory begin with the thinking of the biologist, von Bertalanffy, in the 1920's. Little was done in this area, however, until after the Second World War, when a number of people from various disciplines began to think and write about the *unification* of science. During the succeeding years, several significant conferences, which brought together individuals with these interests, stimulated thinking about systems theory.[2] Then in 1956 a major event occurred with the

[1] For a useful introduction to the perspectives of general systems theory, see Ludwig von Bertalanffy, "General System Theory," *General Systems*, Vol. 1 (1956), pp. 1–10.

[2] The most important of these conferences were a series held at the Michael Reese Hospital in Chicago beginning in October 1951. Thse conferences resulted, among other things, in the following publication: Roy R. Grinker (ed.), *Toward a Unified Theory of Human Behavior* (New York: Basic Books, 1956).

14

General Systems Theory and Political Analysis

founding of the Society for the Advancement of General Systems Research and the publication of its first annual yearbook. Since that time, the Society, which now has several regional chapters, and the yearbook have been the principal focal point for work in the area of general systems theory.

With such an orientation it was natural that people interested in this movement should begin to search for a body of concepts lending unity or organization to studies undertaken in a variety of disciplines and making insights and theoretical advances from individual disciplines widely available. The central and guiding notion that they developed in this quest was the concept of *system,* which has since become a basic conceptual asset of general systems theory. It might therefore be useful to examine several definitions of system in order to acquire a grasp of this starting point. Consider the following definitions:

1. system = a set "of elements standing in interaction."[3]
2. system = "a set of objects together with relationships between the objects and between their attributes."[4]
3. system = "a whole which is compounded of many parts—an ensemble of ATTRIBUTES."[5]

These definitions show a certain genuine continuity and indicate that at least at this high level of abstraction, it is possible to find some real agreement on the notion of system. Each definition embodies the idea of a group of objects or elements standing in some characteristic structural relationships to one another and interacting on the basis of certain characteristic processes. But these general definitions require some elaboration, particularly in regard to the problem of empirical operationalization, in order to pin down the notion of system. In general, it is possible to distinguish two alternative channels that provide ways of handling these problems.

One can take the position that the term system should apply only to elements that are significantly related to each other in the sense that their level of interdependence is high. Here a system would be distinguished from a random aggregation of elements. But this leads to serious problems of operational judgment. Those who follow this approach generally set up criteria such as the following for establishing the existence of a system: (1) a system must be definable in the sense that it can be located with some precision in time and space, (2) a system is spoken of in cases where a

---

[3] von Bertalanffy, *op. cit.,* p. 3.
[4] A. Hall and R. Fagen, "Definition of a System," *General Systems,* Vol. 1 (1956), p. 18.
[5] Colin Cherry, *On Human Communication* (New York: Wiley, 1961). p. 307.

General Systems Theory and Political Analysis

variety of operations carried out preferably by several disciplines arrive at the conclusion that a specific system exists, and (3) a system must manifest significant differences in the time scales of its structures and processes. Such criteria will lead to agreement in the cases of many systems but they are also open to several criticisms. They fail to distinguish adequately between analytic and physical systems or to provide very well for the former.[6] They still leave a certain amount to be desired from the point of view of operationality. And, above all, they do not finally pin down the level of interdependence which forms the breaking point between a random aggregate and a system.

A second approach to these problems has been described as a "constructivist" view of systems.[7] The idea here is that the difficulties mentioned above regarding criteria for the existence of systems are either false problems or else insoluble. The answer therefore is to treat any conglomeration of elements that seems interesting for the purposes of research as a system at least for the preliminary activities of data gathering and initial analysis. Using this approach, any final decision about the existence of a particular system would be made only at a later stage of analysis, at which point the evidence would be sufficient to make a generally acceptable judgment. This approach clearly avoids the necessity of making a number of difficult and sometimes rather arbitrary decisions concerning the existence or nonexistence of systems; but it leaves the analyst with serious problems in grouping his material and discriminating among data during the early phases of his work. And it does not ultimately allow for the avoidance of the problem of making certain judgments concerning the existence or at least relevance of systems.

The originators of general systems theory argued that a great variety of disciplines must deal at a basic level with systems of one kind or another and that there must be certain fundamental though highly abstract orienting concepts relevant to systems of all kinds. This feeling led in turn to the elaboration of the concepts of *isomorphism* and interlocking systems, which have since become basic to the development of general systems theory. In a broad sense, the central point is that systems which differ in terms of size, time scale, and specific substance may yet resemble one another closely in regard to certain basic structures and processes and may also have significant subsets of such structures and processes that interlock.

The concept of *isomorphism* has been defined as "A one-to-one correspondence between objects in different systems which preserves the

---

[6] A physical system is one whose components are concrete entities; an analytic system is an intellectual construct composed of aspects or attributes of concrete entities.

[7] David Easton, *A Framework for Political Analysis* (Englewood Cliffs, N.J.: Prentice-Hall, 1965), pp. 30–34.

General Systems Theory and Political Analysis

relationship between the objects."[8] An isomorphism is therefore more than an analogy since it refers to relationships that are closer than simple likenesses or partial similarities. In this sense, the notion of *homology* corresponds more nearly with the meaning of isomorphism in general systems theory. Both concepts can refer to important structural correspondences across systems. But the notion of isomorphism has a broader reference than that of homology. In fact, from the standpoint of general systems theory the most important isomorphisms are functional (rather than structural) correspondences across systems or fundamental similarities in the governing principles or processes of systems, and not homologies at all.

Interlocking systems and system components, on the other hand, refer more directly to scale effects and to the vertical or hierarchical association of systems. A set of elements forming a significant system in themselves may also constitute a subset of a broader-scale system or possess subsets that are identical with those of one or more additional systems. In this context the discovery of interlocking relationships amongst a variety of systems tends to be an important factor in analyzing both individual systems and sets of systems.

The basic concepts of isomorphism and interlocking systems suggest very strongly that there are important concepts and propositions that are meaningful over a significant range of specific systems and that it is possible to develop in conceptual terms a small number of general systems. These notions together with the fundamental concept of system now form the heart of the campaign aimed at breaking down the compartmentalization of disciplines and moving toward the unification of science. General systems theory constitutes a record of efforts to elaborate basic principles relevant to a wide range of systems and to develop techniques for applying these principles to the specific and concrete systems of interest to various fields of research.

This reference to basic principles suggests a brief discussion of the substantive nature of general systems theory. Limitations of space make it impossible to set forth an inventory of the propositions involved in general systems theory, but some comment on its principal concepts may be useful at this point to clarify the theory's substantive scope and to give some indication of the perspectives generated by the systemic point of view.[9] The relevant concepts divide into several major groups.

First, some concepts are primarily descriptive. The concepts in this group suggest important distinctions, classify large quantities of data in

[8] Hall and Fagen, *op. cit.*, p. 24.
[9] For further elaboration see O. R. Young, "A Survey of General Systems Theory," *General Systems*, Vol. 9 (1964), pp. 61–80.

General Systems Theory and Political Analysis

relevant ways, and outline the basic structure and processes of various types of system. Within this group, several relevant subcategories suggest themselves on the basis of their subject matter: (1) concepts that separate different kinds of system such as open and closed systems or organismic and nonorganismic systems, (2) concepts concerning hierarchical levels of systems such as subsystem, orders of interaction, and scale effects, (3) concepts delineating aspects of the internal organization of systems such as integration, differentiation, interdependence, and centralization, (4) concepts related to the interaction of systems with their environments such as boundaries, inputs and outputs, and (5) concepts dealing with the various paths which systems may follow over time such as state-determinedness and equifinality.

Beyond these essentially descriptive and classificatory variables, there are several additional groups of concepts central to general systems theory. A second group of concepts focuses on factors that *regulate* and *maintain* systems. On the one hand, this group includes the intricate and frequently somewhat confused concepts that center on the notions of stability, equilibrium, and homeostasis. On the other hand, it also encompasses a number of process variables such as feedback in several of its forms, repair and reproduction, and entropy in its negative, but not its positive, form. The central theme of this group is the modes and means through which various systems maintain their essential elements within the bounds of recognizability.

The rest of the core concepts of systems theory deal with questions that arise when systems do not maintain themselves without significant changes in their basic patterns. A third group focuses on dynamics. Here the principal questions deal with nondisruptive change either through internally generated processes or through responses to altered environmental conditions. Change itself can be usefully divided into reversible and irreversible developments. But in this group the main focus is on concepts such as adaptation, learning, and growth. Also included at this point are the notions of systemic purposes, goals, and teleology. Nondisruptive change is not, however, the only channel along which systems that do not maintain themselves unchanged can move. A final group of general systems concepts emphasizes phenomena such as disruption, dissolution, and breakdown in systems. Relevant here are the notions of systemic crisis, stress and strain. The concepts of overload and decay represent two forms in which breakdown or dissolution may appear. And the famous "law" of positive entropy takes its place in the conceptual framework at this point.[10]

[10] This is the second law of thermodynamics which states that, all other things being equal, individual elements in a group of elements will tend to seek their most probable distribution over time (i.e., array themselves randomly).

General Systems Theory and Political Analysis

Taken together, these conceptual patterns and the propositions built upon them constitute the body of general systems theory. But as is frequently the case with theoretical material at this high level of abstraction, there are two fundamental points of view concerning the basic nature of systems theory. From one standpoint, general systems theory appears as an integrated and generalized set of concepts, hypotheses, and (hopefully as time passes) validated propositions. In this context the maximum hope for the theory is the establishment of an integrated set of high-level theoretical principles dealing with all or almost all of the significant elements of a small number of inclusive general systems and applicable to important phenomena in a wide range of disciplines. With this view one would measure the progress of systems theory in terms of advancement toward that goal. On the other hand, general systems theory may be seen as a set of techniques and as a framework for a systematic process of analysis. In this instance it is not so much the specific principles and propositions of the theory that are of ultimate interest; rather it is the suggestions that the theory offers for analyzing and organizing data, the insights derivable from the use of the notion of isomorphisms, the richness of the concepts, and the value of the framework of systems theory for purposes of coding large amounts of data which are significant. From this vantage point the worth of systems theory is calculated in terms of its utility in performing the functions just outlined rather than in terms of any ideal theoretical goal. Each of these points of view is valid. Although it is perhaps true that the notion of systems theory as a framework for an analytic process is more in line with scientific method and offers more scope for the application of the theory, the successful development of a series of general systems principles would have very great value for many disciplines.

General systems theory is especially oriented toward systematic empirical analysis in several respects. It provides a source of concepts and working models that offer considerable hope for empirical operationalization and that can be applied to a great many specific, substantive areas in order to generate empirically verifiable hypotheses. In this sense, the underlying thrust of the theory makes it attractive from the standpoint of empirical research. In addition, the potential utility of general systems theory in standardizing terminology, coding data, and storing information is highly relevant to some of the important problems of empirical analysis. But above all, the communication and transfer of insights along the channels of isomorphisms and interlocking systems have provided a real impetus for empirical work. In this connection, systems theory has become associated with the increasing use of the advances of recent years in mathematical and computational techniques. In particular, the channels of ismorphisms have given a number of fields important computational models and concepts

General Systems Theory and Political Analysis

useful for the exploitation of a wide range of technological advances in the realm of mathematical analysis.

Functions of General Systems Theory in Political Analysis

Before discussing general systems theory in terms of the types of approach to political analysis outlined in Chapter One, it is important to say a few words about the use of general systems concepts in political science. General systems theory in its extended and well-integrated form has very rarely been applied to the analysis of political phenomena. To do so would require a high level of theoretical consciousness as well as a substantial program of systematic and somewhat abstract analysis. Furthermore, it is true even now that the basic conceptual and propositional materials of systems theory remain largely undistilled and are therefore not available without a great deal of searching through a somewhat disconnected body of literature. A number of central concepts of the theory, however, have become extremely popular in recent years with the result that they are now used rather indiscriminately in a wide variety of contexts. This is especially true of the notion of system which is applied freely to virtually any set of related behavior patterns, but it is also true to a lesser extent of such other concepts as stability, feedback, and even entropy. As David Easton points out in a recent discussion of the notion of system, "In most cases it is just a handy notion, popular and apparently simple, to refer to the range of phenomena that in earlier days might have roused a different terminology, such as politics, government, or the state."[11] As a result, the application of general systems theory proper constitutes a notably different type of approach to analysis than the looser and more informal usage of common practice.

In its looser manifestation systems theory can be largely equated with the type of approach illustrated by Merton's suggestions concerning *general orientations*. The hope here is that the employment of certain concepts and perspectives from systems theory will lift the study of political phenomena above the older channels worn by more familiar approaches and in so doing suggest fresh frames of reference and insight. This is, in fact, a valid and potentially profitable enterprise but it should not be confused with the utilization of general systems theory proper in its more extended form. As an approach to analysis, the latter is much closer to being an example of Easton's notion of *conceptual frameworks*. Although the propositions of systems theory, in particular, are somewhat scattered and buried in the relevant literature, the theory does ultimately support a rather impressive analytic superstructure. And this superstructure is made all the more

[11] Easton, *op. cit.*, p. 26.

General Systems Theory and Political Analysis

ambitious by general systems theory's objective of developing a set of basic principles applicable to a wide range of empirical systems.

There is a sense in which general systems theory is somewhat broader in scope than the other approaches discussed in this volume. The basic reason for this stems from the fact that systems theory has been formulated on a very high level of abstraction both in order to make it applicable to a variety of disciplines and in order to give it the capacity to serve as a housing for middle- and lower-range theories in specific disciplines. At the present time, a body of theory aimed at performing this framework function is of considerable value for political analysis. Theory of this kind is useful in emphasizing the complementary qualities of various approaches to political analysis, which have characteristically been placed in opposition to each other. In addition, a general systems framework should also aid in clarifying the extent of redundancy in theories that are essentially stylistic variations of one another.

Utilizing the breakdown of the subject matter of political science outlined in Chapter One, we may outline several areas in which general systems theory appears to be particularly promising.[12] A factor that should be singled out, above all, is the extensiveness and richness of the descriptive concepts and categories of systems theory. The use of this approach is frequently of great value in sorting out a large quantity of data and in recognizing the patterns and uniformities that tie elements of a system together. For example, the designation of a system as being *open,* in the sense of exchanging inputs and outputs with an environment, or *closed,* sets in motion a series of related inquiries. Boundary questions are of primary significance in dealing with open systems, positive entropy applies principally to closed systems, and so forth. A notion such as differentiation is productive in much the same sense. If the components of a system are highly differentiated, for example, this tends to touch off inquiries concerning levels of decentralization and, as a consequence, the role of leading parts.

A second realm in which systems theory is quite useful encompasses the area of pattern maintenance variables. Notions such as stability and, especially, equilibrium have, of course, been employed rather frequently, if somewhat loosely, in the literature of political science. But general systems theory goes considerably beyond common usage in this area in several respects. To begin with, the concepts are made more precise and are placed in the context of a more general theory. In addition, they are further elaborated in the framework of systems theory and buttressed by related

[12] For further suggestions on this subject consult O. R. Young, "The Impact of General Systems Theory on Political Science," *General Systems,* Vol. 9 (1964), especially pp. 249–253.

General Systems Theory and Political Analysis

concepts. Stability, for example, is a much more complex phenomenon in the case of an open system than in the case of a closed one. Equilibrium may be stable or unstable, and stability itself can be resolved at least into the cases of immediate or proximate stability and ultrastability.[13] Then too, much of the interest in pattern maintenance is directed to processes and actions rather than to end results. And here the material from general systems theory built around the notions of feedback, control, homeostatic mechanisms, repair, and reproduction is particularly useful.

Beyond this, systems theory provides an explicit framework for the inclusion of material concerning change and systemic breakdown, an area that has been somewhat neglected in modern political analysis. It is not necessary to disagree entirely with Easton's argument[14] that political systems rarely break down or disintegrate utterly in order to argue that much more attention should be paid to the problems of systemic pathologies, crises, and tendencies toward dissolution. There are different basic types of crisis, for example, and it makes a substantial difference whether the essential problem is one of overload or "starvation."[15] And breakdown based on the centrifugal pressures of positive entropy is a different phenomenon than dissolution caused by the decay of a critical systemic process. Even in cases where systems do not ultimately break down, therefore, the study of these variables may shed a great deal of light on various deficiencies in performance levels that are, in fact, very common. Moreover, it may very well be possible to acquire some insights concerning the processes through which systems adapt to altered conditions resulting both from endogenous and exogenous change.

The functions of general systems theory for political analysis can also be conceptualized along another, somewhat more abstract, axis. The effectiveness of this approach for systematic empirical analysis has already become apparent in a general way and should be kept in mind from the point of view of applying systems theory to political analysis as well. In this more abstract discussion of functions, we should also add that general systems theory often facilitates the communication of insights and ways of looking at things from other disciplines. This function stems largely from the concept of isomorphism and from the systems theory objective of breaking down barriers of compartmentalization. The discipline of political science is presently at a stage where it can benefit substantially from a consideration of theoretical problems, techniques of conceptualization, and

[13] See W. Ross Ashby, *Design for a Brain* (New York: Wiley, 1952), pp. 90–102.

[14] Easton, *op. cit.*, Chapter VI.

[15] A "starvation" crisis ensues when the inputs into a system are insufficient for the maintenance of a given level of performance. For example, an automobile which runs out of fuel will not function.

General Systems Theory and Political Analysis

methods of overcoming various difficulties of analysis in other disciplines, as well as from direct insights that may be wholly or partially transferred to political problems. General systems theory provides excellent channels for maximizing the flow of such interchanges even with disciplines that are sometimes considered far removed from political science in substantive terms.

Somewhat analogous to the preceding function is another type of transfer activity that general systems theory facilitates. Knowledge, insights, and fruitful questions can be transferred from one system level to another as well as across discipline lines, and therefore from one substantive type of system to another. Thus, for example, it is sometimes possible to study large-scale systems by transferring knowledge or techniques acquired in the analysis of very small systems or of a variety of subsystems. And there are reverse cases in which large systems can serve as prototypes for very small systems that are difficult to study independently.

In general, systems theory is probably more useful for problems of macroanalysis than for problems of microanalysis. By its very nature this body of theory provides an excellent framework for the classification and analysis of rather large aggregates of data. In addition, it is well organized for the study of complete functioning entities as contrasted with individual elements or contributory factors. This is not to say that systems theory must be used only for very broad-gauge or overarching studies; it has been applied with interesting results to such matters as psychic pathologies in human beings. In the analysis of political phenomena, however, the fact that systems are taken as the basic units of analysis tends to focus attention on the macro aspects of political systems whether they exist at the local, national, regional, or international level.

Finally, it is worth mentioning that general systems theory contains a number of remarkably clear and precise ways of formulating concepts that exist, for the most part, in other analytical systems but in a more nebulous form. In this sense the approach may have some didactic functions over and above its utility for the pursuit of pure research. In the case of systems theory this quality probably stems from the fact that the concepts involved can frequently be reduced to an operational form and that, in most cases, they are easily illustrated with very sharp examples.

To round out this picture it is necessary to comment on substantive areas in which general systems theory seems either largely irrelevant or applicable only in a less fruitful way than alternative approaches to analysis. When this result occurs it usually stems from a lack of conceptual richness needed to develop thought-provoking distinctions and to order large quantities of data, and from a subsequent poverty in the extent to which the approach generates hypotheses concerning a given substantive   **23** area. This situation may be made clear most easily by means of several examples. Systems theory has only a limited amount to offer for studies of political power and influence. Although it does consider the systemwide impact of various kinds of control mechanism, it lacks the apparatus to deal extensively with such questions as the scope, depth, and weight of power. Moreover, the use of the system as the basic unit of analysis makes it difficult to conceptualize in any detail questions concerning the strategy and tactics of employing power and influence. A second and related example encompasses the kinds of phenomena that are of interest to analysts who pursue a more psychological approach to political behavior. Although systems theory may be helpful in organizing material on human relationships into systemic patterns in such a way that questions concerning pattern maintenance, stability, regulation, and so forth can be posed fruitfully, it does not have as much to offer for studies dealing with the political aspects of such matters as perception, expectation formation, or cognition. Or again, general systems theory is of only limited utility in studies of political policy making. While it may aid considerably in conceptualizing and analyzing the actual operations of a decision-making system, it has little to say about goal formation and it does not address itself to the problems of generating alternative sets of concrete policies. To lend perspective to these examples the point should also be made that there are additional substantive areas in which both systems theory and one or more other approaches may, upon application, yield differing but equally interesting and useful insights.

Criticisms and Problems

A number of significant criticisms of general systems theory have appeared in the literature in recent years. In this short space, it is possible to outline only the most important criticisms and to point out a few of the limitations of the criticisms themselves.

There is some controversy over the content of the notion *isomorphism*. Some critics maintain that, in actuality, there are not very many significant isomorphic relationships and that systems theory's demand for isomorphisms sometimes leads to a practice of forcing things into "boxes" in which they do not belong. This is ultimately an empirical question that cannot be fully resolved on an abstract or deductive basis. It is relatively clear that a number of isomorphic relationships do exist and that the conceptual notion of isomorphism is not entirely empty empirically. The important question, however, concerns criteria of significance with which to judge isomorphic relationships. And it is difficult to be very sure of such criteria in the absence of more extensive empirical applications of the

24

concepts and hypotheses of general systems theory. Nevertheless, the criticism raised here is one with rather far-reaching implications since the notion of isomorphism is very important to the central thrust of systems theory.

In a somewhat related fashion, there are those who argue that the conceptual categories of systems theory lead analysts to force all phenomena into the framework of a system. There are two ways of treating this problem, depending upon one's choice between the alternative methods of pinning down the notion of system, outlined earlier. The "constructivist" viewpoint suggests that it is possible to postulate that "any set of variables selected for description and explanation may be considered a system of behavior."[16] Judgments about significance would come only later. The other viewpoint relies on a set of criteria applicable to any universe of data and that serve as the operational means of separating significant systems from random groups of variables. This general problem is clearly of some importance, though it is also relevant to point out that in many systemic analyses the designation of systems would probably only be controversial in various marginal cases.

There is also some criticism of general systems theory that suggests it constitutes an elaborate and abstract conceptual structure that is lacking when it comes to hypotheses and propositions. This is not, of course, a fully meaningful criticism from the point of view of all of the types of approach outlined in Chapter One. In any case, the fact is that general systems theory does support a good many hypotheses and propositions of an abstract nature. Although this material tends to be buried in the literature and therefore somewhat obscured, a careful reading of the principal writings in this area will turn up a substantial quantity of hypotheses and propositions. In regard to the problem of levels of abstraction, there are those who allege that there is an inevitable trade-off between rising levels of abstraction and decreasing content or meaning. But this is not necessarily true. Abstractions sometimes serve to summarize essential conceptual problems and sets of relationships that stand in an antecedent relationship to the whole question of specific content. Above all, however, there are numerous cases in which it is necessary to raise levels of abstraction in order to give meaning and content to a group of elements or variables that do not appear to be significantly related when discussed at a lower level of abstraction.

Like all approaches to analysis, general systems theory also throws up certain snags in regard to problems of empirical operationalization. The question here involves the provision of operational indices for the empirical application of concepts and propositions. The difficulties surrounding the very notion of system itself have cropped up at several points in this

[16] Easton, *op. cit.*, p. 30.

General Systems Theory and Political Analysis

discussion. Moreover, there are some special aspects of the problem of operationalization when general systems theory is applied to the social sciences. The distinction between open and closed systems sometimes begins to blur, boundaries are difficult to place especially in temporal sequences, and "analytic" systems must often be separated from tangible, physical systems.[17] Taken together, these problems appear to be at least as manageable as the problems of operationalizing most other approaches. In the end, it is the fact that general systems theory has come sufficiently close to being operational (making the necessary adjustments worth working on) that makes the problem of operationalization relevant at all to this discussion.

Finally, it is important to remember that general systems theory proper has been utilized very little in the social sciences and that it is therefore difficult to judge its utility at this time. Moreover, existing work tends very often to address itself more to the general elaboration of the approach than to empirical applications. This is not actually a criticism of the theory so much as a reservation. General systems theory may achieve a high standing as an approach to political analysis, but it is too early to make any definitive judgments on this question.

[17] For this last distinction see *Ibid.*, pp. 37–44.

General Systems Theory and Political Analysis

Systems

Derivatives

This chapter focuses on the systemic approaches to analysis
that have attracted a considerable amount of attention
from political scientists. Interestingly, these approaches have
more often been adapted to the needs of political analysis from other
disciplines than generated by political scientists
themselves. In a conceptual and theoretical
sense, all of the systemic approaches derive from the basic
framework of general systems theory, although in fact some of them
chronologically antedate the bulk of the work on general

systems theory. The present chapter deals at some length with two of the most influential systemic approaches: (1) *structural functionalism* and (2) *input-output analysis*.

Structural-Functional Analysis

The basic unit of analysis for structural functionalism is always a system or set of interlocking systems just as it is in general systems theory. In the analysis of social and political phenomena, the term system also carries most of the same general connotations and nuances for the two approaches. Moreover, at this fundamental level there are additional links between the two modes of analysis. In Marion Levy's terms, structural-functional analysis proceeds from the definition of the unit to the elaboration of its "setting."[1] These considerations correspond very closely to the definition of a system and the discussion of its environment and boundary conditions that are characteristic of analysis under the general systems approach. In addition, both forms of analysis are very much concerned with questions focusing on differences between relevant system levels, the reciprocal influences of various system levels on one another, and the implications of these factors for the levels of generalization and abstraction at which particular analyses are formulated. Finally, it is probably fair to say that the most fundamental concern of structural-functional analysis is with the phenomena of system maintenance and regulation. In this connection especially, the nature of structural functionalism as a conceptual derivative of general systems theory becomes apparent.

Structural-functional analysis in its contemporary, systematic form stems from the work of the anthropologists, Malinowski and Radcliffe-Brown, in the early decades of this century. The field of sociology subsequently adopted and refined the mode of analysis, which has since become a major sociological framework in terms of the uses to which it has been put. Especially since the 1950's a number of political scientists have begun to apply adapted versions of structural functionalism to various problems of political analysis. This tendency has been particularly noticeable in the field of comparative politics, although it has not been absent in other branches of the discipline of political science.

The conceptual framework of the structural-functional approach centers around the question, What structures fulfill what basic functions and under what conditions in any given system? This general question contains several terms requiring some clarification, and this necessity

[1] Marion Levy, Jr., *The Structure of Society* (Princeton, N.J.: Princeton University Press, 1952), pp. 36–38.

Systems Derivatives

provides a good starting point from which to move into the substance of the structural-functional approach. The single concept that is most basic to the approach is that of function in its *broadest* sense. There is a good deal of terminological confusion surrounding this concept in the literature; difficulties are often raised by efforts to pin down the nature of a function alternatively as an objective, a process, or a result. In a general sense, however, a function may be defined as the objective consequence(s) of a pattern of action for the system (in this case social or political) in which it occurs. Starting from this definition, it is clear that the problems raised above are not very substantial. Functions deal ultimately with objective consequences, but they may be perceived as objectives, processes, or results from various points of view and for various purposes. A given function may therefore be examined from each of these points of view for specific purposes, although none of them reaches the essence of the concept.

Within this broad meaning of the concept function, a number of more specific distinctions are important. Above all, a distinction is generally drawn between functions (or *eufunctions* in Levy's terminology) and *dysfunctions*. As Robert Merton puts it, "*Functions* are those observed consequences which make for the adaptation or adjustment of a given system; and *dysfunctions,* those observed consequences which lessen the adaptation or adjustment of the system."[2] In this connection it is important to note that the same patterns of action may simultaneously produce functional and dysfunctional consequences. Such a result is quite possible at any given system level, and it is a rather common occurrence when varying system levels are taken into account. It is not uncommon, for example, to find patterns of consequences that are functional for the over-all social system but dysfunctional for many individual human beings, or *vice versa*. For these reasons it is necessary to analyze systemic patterns of action in terms of the balances of functional and dysfunctional consequences which they produce.[3]

Another important distinction separates *manifest* and *latent* functions. Following Merton's analysis, the key variables in this distinction are *intent* and *recognition*.[4] A manifest function deals with patterns of action whose consequence are both intended and recognized by the participants, while latent functions cover patterns whose consequences are unintended and

[2] Robert K. Merton, *Social Theory and Social Structure* (Glencoe, Ill.: The Free Press, 1957), p. 51.

[3] Some proponents of structural functionalism also speak of nonfunctional phenomena, i.e., phenomena that produce neither functional nor dysfunctional consequences. Levy, on the other hand, argues that "The concept of non-function . . . is inutile." See his "Structural-Functional Analysis," mimeographed version of an article for the *International Encyclopedia of the Social Sciences* (Princeton, N.J.: Princeton University, 1965), p. 14.

[4] Merton, *op. cit.,* pp. 60–82.

unrecognized by the participants.[5] Merton argues that in empirical terms the class of latent functions in most social systems is a very large one since most patterns of action have many consequences in addition to their intended and recognized ones. He also suggests that the most important task of the scholar concerns the analysis of latent functions. Manifest functions are clear-cut and well recognized. Latent functions, however, are numerous, highly complex, and unlikely to be analyzed seriously by anyone other than the scholar.

The other principal element of the basic question of structural-functional analysis focuses on structures. While functions concern the consequences of patterns of action, structures refer to the patterns of action and resultant institutions of the system themselves. Functions are therefore performed by various structural arrangements in any given system. But there are a number of additional distinctions that must be made here too. It is frequently the case that a variety of specific, manifest structures can fulfill any basic function. Moreover, there is no one-to-one correspondence between functions and structures. Just as a single function may be fulfilled by a complex combination of structures, any given structural arrangement may have functional or dysfunctional consequences for a variety of functions. Early functional analysis tended to insist on the so-called postulate of indispensability, which states that every empirically present pattern of action (i.e., structure) in a system must fulfill or contribute positively to the fulfillment of a vital function.[6] This postulate has since given way to a much more detailed and satisfactory analysis that is symbolized by the somewhat confusingly labeled concept of functional equivalents or alternatives. This concept codifies the proposition that a given function can be fulfilled by many different structural arrangements and might perhaps be labeled more descriptively as the concept of structural substitutability. The incorporation of this concept into the approach performs the valuable role of alerting the analyst to the wide variety of structural alternatives that exist in most systems. There are, of course, limits to this systemic malleability, a fact that is usually discussed under the concept of contextual constraints. In real situations large numbers of specific structures are woven together to form the prevailing pattern of social institutions at any given time. The resulting interdependencies place sharp limitations on the amount of structural change that can be wrought without significantly affecting a wide variety of additional structures in the system and ultimately throwing the whole system into flux.

[5] Levy also distinguishes several intermediate patterns. These include functions that are unintended but recognized (UIR) and intended but unrecognized (IUR). In addition, Levy applies the manifest-latent distinction to structures as well as to functions. See Levy, "Structural-Functional Analysis," *op. cit.*, pp. 17 *ff.*

[6] Merton, *op. cit.*, pp. 32–36.

Systems Derivatives

Within this over-all framework a number of additional categories and distinctions assume increasing importance. A great deal of work in the field of structural-functional anlysis focuses on questions concerning functional requisites or requirements.[7] In this connection analysis tends to start from the proposition that any given system will have certain "conditions of survival" where survival is taken to mean the maintenance of the essential characteristics of the system within the bounds of recognizability. Although there may be a great variation in structural arrangements, many analysts believe that it is possible to distinguish and pin down a finite set of functions that must be fulfilled if a given system or class of systems is to survive. Some treatments insist on a defined and numerically specific set of functional requisites, while others are more flexible and open-ended on this point. In addition, it is possible to insist on a specific set of functional requisites for a class of systems at a rather high level of abstraction and still allow for a certain amount of variation when it comes to the analysis of particular cases within this class. Levy, for example, discusses the functional requisites of *any* social system on a very abstract basis and comes up with a list of ten required functions.[8]

The problem of functional requisites has generated a number of questions concerning various specific types of requisite. In recent years considerable effort has been expended in constructing taxonomies of functional requisites for various types of systems. The utilization of structural-functional analysis by political scientists is just now reaching this stage and the question of alternative types of requisites is presently a very live one. Gabriel Almond, for instance, has recently set forth an extended scheme in this area involving conversion functions, capabilities functions, and adaptation and maintenance functions as the functional requirements of a political system.[9] Others are actively working on alternative formulations. There are essentially two approaches to the construction of such taxonomies: (1) the logical partition which forms a conclusive list, and (2) the open-ended and expandable listing. Unfortunately there are serious difficulties with both procedures that tend to cast doubt on the usefulness of expending major efforts along these lines. A logical partition is a precise construction in logical terms, but by its very nature it is based on one variable or set of variables with the result that alternative lists of functions

---

[7] Some analysts have also worked with the concept of structural requisites. This notion, however, has received far less attention than the concept of functional requisites.

[8] Levy, 1952, *op. cit.*, Chapter IV.

[9] Gabriel Almond, "A Developmental Approach to Political Systems," *World Politics,* Vol. XVII, No. 2 (January 1965), pp. 183–214. For Almond's earlier thoughts on functional requisites, consult also Gabriel Almond and James S. Coleman (eds.), *The Politics of the Developing Areas* (Princeton, N.J.: Princeton University Press, 1960), Chapter I.

based on other axes will invariably be offered. And there is no way of making a final selection among such alternatives. An open-ended list, on the other hand, is not very satisfactory either since it leaves the analyst with an ambiguous and often amorphous conceptual tool around which it is difficult to structure research. Lists of this kind, moreover, tend to change quite rapidly, with the result that they are of very dubious value for serious, systematic analysis.

Much of structural-functional analysis tends to focus primarily on essentially static relationships rather than on dynamics. The approach is concerned, above all, with the problems of systemic survival, the requirements of stable adaptation, and the operation of various functions and structures oriented toward system maintenance. This point should not be overemphasized, however, since there are several aspects of structural functionalism that do provide perspectives on change. First, the analysis of structural and functional prerequisites deals with the conditions under which new systems can come into existence. As Levy puts it, these prerequisites refer to structures and functions "that must pre-exist if a given unit in its setting is to come into being."[10] Second, the notion of a changing balance of functions and dysfunctions emanating from a variety of specific structures has important implications for change. In Merton's words, "The concept of dysfunction, which implies the concept of strain, stress and tension on the structural level, provides an analytic approach to the study of dynamics and change."[11] Within an ongoing system, therefore, there is considerable room for the analysis of possible permutations, especially in structural arrangements. In this connection, the restricting concept of contextual constraints can be reversed to open up a discussion of the limits of variability that exist in any given system. Analysis here deals with the amount of change at the structural level that a system can accommodate without seriously hindering the fulfillment of its basic functional requisites.

In initiating the discussion of the uses of the structural-functional approach in political analysis, a few words concerning the basic nature of this approach to analysis will be helpful. The version of structural functionalism outlined in the preceding pages tends toward the general orientation end of the scale of types of approach outlined in Chapter One. Merton has argued correctly that several rather broad theorems or propositions often attributed to structural-functional analysis are, in fact, insupportable.[12] In particular, he demonstrates this conclusion concerning three theorems or, as he labels them, postulates. The "postulate of the

[10] Levy, "Structural-Functional Analysis," *op. cit.*, p. 11.
[11] Merton, *op. cit.*, p. 53.
[12] *Ibid.*, pp. 25–37.

Systems Derivatives

functional unity of society" suggests that all social systems are highly integrated and that every pattern of action has some close functional tie-in to the operation of the system. This proposition is simply false empirically. The "postulate of universal functionalism" asserts "that all standardized social or cultural forms have positive functions."[13] This position breaks down in reality in the face of dysfunctional patterns of action. Finally, the "postulate of indispensability" has two forms: it is sometimes used to assert that a certain function is indispensable to the maintenance of a social or political system, while at other times it is used to argue for the necessity of some particular structural arrangements. Earlier discussion in this chapter indicated that the notion of certain functional requisites is an important (though controversial) one, but in many cases the notion of structural necessity goes squarely against increasing evidence in favor of the view that the scope for structural alternatives is substantial in most systems. All of this leaves an approach that is based primarily on the important role of providing a general orientation. Even in Merton's version, however, it should be added that there are still some important (though often implicit) propositions incorporated into the structural-functional approach. It is agreed, for example, that there are almost certainly at least some functional requisites for any given system. And most would agree with the proposition that almost all systems, and especially social systems, show very substantial scope for structural substitution within their limits of variability.

As far as political analysis is concerned, the structural-functional approach appears to offer several advantages: It is quite attractive for comparative analysis of political systems; it deals for the most part with a manageable collection of variables; and it provides a set of standardized categories that can be applied successfully over widely disparate political systems. This interest in the approach for comparative work, for example, is clearly a major factor explaining the amount of effort now being expended by political scientists on the elaboration of taxonomies of types of function. An important factor in this connection is the fact that the approach rests on a rather abstract analysis of the general conception of a social system and that it is stated in such a way as to be able to handle substantial variations at more specific levels of analysis. An example of this advantage appears in Levy's abstract formulation of functional requisite analysis for *any* society followed by particular applications and adaptations to specific social systems.

In terms of the categories of political analysis elaborated in Chapter One, the structural-functional approach is somewhat selective but of substantial interest in the particular areas of its emphasis. Its categories and concepts are less broad in terms of scope than those of general systems

[13] *Ibid.*, p. 30.

theory, but they provide considerable richness for purposes of orientation and data selection in their own domain. The greatest strength of the structual-functional approach lies in the area of pattern maintainence and systemic regulation. Here the essentially static elements of the approach display themselves to best advantage. The approach focuses its substantial conceptual apparatus on such matters as the conditions of "survival" of any given system; the structures and institutional mechanisms through which basic requirements for systemic maintainence are fulfilled; the balances of functional and dysfunctional consequences of various patterns of action calculated in terms of impetus to change structural arrangements; and the methods by which certain specific conditions leading to systemic termination can be avoided. It is therefore not surprising that the approach has seemed important to many analysts pursuing the study of on-going and, especially, rather slowly changing political systems, and that it has lent itself to the needs of comparative political analysis in the earlier stages of its development.

At the same time, the structural-functional approach lacks conceptual facilities to deal in a very detailed manner with questions arising in certain other segments of political analysis. Variables concerning patterns of control are not central to the approach. The phenomena of power and influence, for example, are likely to be brought in only on a very secondary level in discussions of such matters as the specific patterns for fulfilling certain functional requisites. Moreover, this type of analysis provides relatively little scope for the discussion of goals and objectives. Its emphasis on maintainence and survival (though these are systemic goals in themselves) tends to circumscribe the extent to which it can deal with other types of normative demands and interests. In terms of policy studies, for example, structural functionalism may be a useful adjunct but it can hardly provide the basic framework for analysis.

In recent years structural functionalism has suffered much heavy criticism, especially from a number of sociologists who have worked with the approach for some time and who have now become more and more aware of its disadvantages. Criticism from political scientists is considerably less virulent since the approach has only in recent years become common currency in the discipline. Interestingly enough, a good deal of the criticism leveled at the approach deserves ultimately to revert to some of its practitioners rather than to be attributed to the intrinsic nature of the approach itself. It is true that structural functionalism generates several pitfalls, but the skilled practitioner can frequently find ways to circumvent such difficulties.

To begin with, the structural-functional approach is criticized, just as general systems theory is, for a tendency to force divergent phenomena into

Systems Derivatives

a systemic framework even though they do not always fit. This criticism, however, is essentially marginal in its implications since few will argue against the systemic nature of a great many phenomena. It is only the marginal cases, therefore, that are really controversial. What does seem to be true, however, is that the constructivist approach to systems discussed in Chapter Two is more difficult to apply in the case of structural functionalism than in the case of general systems theory. The decision to go ahead with a structural-functional analysis tends to demand that a clear judgment already be made to the effect that a significant system exists, thereby making it more difficult to exercise the ex post facto judgment called for by the constructivist approach.

There are several common criticisms of the structural-functional approach that deal with the relationships between functions and structures. The "fallacy of functional teleology"[14] refers to the tendency to explain the origins of a condition or pattern of action in terms of its being a functional necessity for the survival of the system. The fact, however, that a particular structural arrangement fulfills an important function is not an adequate explanation of its origin or existence. In any given situation there are likely to be a number of alternative forms that could play the same role so that a particular pattern of action is not absolutely indispensable. A second criticism concerns the postulate of universal functionalism, which as explained above suggests that all existing structures fulfill or partially fulfill a vital function. This proposition overlooks the importance of dysfunctional consequences and systemic "survivals"[15] as well as the extensive possibilities of structural alternatives in most systems. Both of these pitfalls have created serious problems for many analysts utilizing the structural-functional approach, and a number of studies are quite seriously compromised due to the resultant difficulties. Nevertheless, it is important to notice that both problems are avoidable without obviating the approach and in most cases by means of a constructive reformulation, as Merton demonstrates in the case of the problem of functional teleology. The full force of the criticism, therefore, applies more to certain practitioners than to the approach itself.

Essentially the same can be said of the fallacy of deductive functionalism. A number of analysts using the structural-functional approach have

[14] Levy, 1952, op. cit., pp. 52–54.

[15] The notion of survivals refers here to structural arrangements that formerly fulfilled a function but that have lost all or part of their functional significance in the course of the evolution of a system over time. The work of Abram Kardiner contains the most systematic exposition of this concept. For detailed formulations see Abram Kardiner, The Individual and His Society (New York: Columbia University Press, 1939), and Abram Kardiner, The Psychological Frontiers of Society (New York: Columbia University Press, 1945).

Systems Derivatives

shown a strong tendency to develop deductively a list of functional requisites and then to make sure to find structural patterns which fulfill these requisites. This leads quite commonly to an unwarranted twisting and distorting of empirical realities in the interests of conceptual and theoretical neatness. This, however, is a problem common to much intellectual endeavor and does not imply an intrinsic inadequacy of the structural-functional approach. While the resultant difficulties have not infrequently cropped up in specific structural-functional analyses, they are primarily the responsibility of individual practitioners.

A further criticism charges that structural functionalism is essentially a static system of analysis. As suggested earlier, the strongest elements of the approach do, in fact, deal with matters such as requisite analysis in which a stability assumption[16] is often made for analytic (not evaluative) purposes. At the same time, the approach does offer some perspectives on change that merit serious consideration. To the extent that there is a criticism of structural functionalism to be made in this area, it should be treated more as a relevant limitation than as a critical inadequacy of the approach.

One of the most damning of the criticisms frequently leveled against the structural-functional approach is that it has serious ideological implications[17] and in particular that it tends to lead to the rationalization and/or justification of the *status quo*. The idea here is that the approach leads to a defense of the existing order of things by purporting to demonstrate the functionality of existing patterns. This is especially evident in the earlier functional schemes that insisted on the theorems that Merton has labeled the postulates of universal functionalism and of indispensability. Such postulates actually do tend to insist on the essential nature of existing patterns and to lend support to the view that what is is somehow good. As suggested in the preceding pages, however, postulates of this kind are neither supportable nor central to contemporary structural-functional analysis. Merton has also argued interestingly that it is possible to accuse structural functionalism of harboring a radical bias essentially on the grounds that it is somewhat mechanistic and lends itself to ideas concerning experiments in social engineering. As with some of the other criticisms, however, this one concerning ideology should be directed more specifically toward the practitioners in the field than toward the approach itself. It is quite possible to conduct an analysis utilizing the structural-functional approach without being influenced by ideological considerations, even though it is an empirical fact that many analysts have included ideological biases in analyses based on this approach. On balance, it is fair to say that

---

[16] Levy, "Structural-Functional Analysis," *op. cit.*, p. 8.
[17] For an interesting discussion, see Merton, *op. cit.*, pp. 37–42.

Systems Derivatives

the nature of the approach makes it relatively easy to slip into "conservative" patterns and biases without much thought and that special care should be taken to avoid that pitfall. This is, therefore, a real problem, but it is not the same one that would arise if a substantial ideological bias were inextricably incorporated into the structural-functional approach itself.

Input-Output Analysis

A second major systemic approach stems largely from the work of David Easton, a political scientist who has been interested in the problems of approaches to analysis for some years. As such, the approach is one of the few systemic frameworks originally developed by a political scientist rather than adapted for political analysis from some other discipline. In input-output analysis the focus is again on the system as the basic unit of analysis and on the intrasystem and intersystem behavior of various systems as principal areas for research. As Easton himself says in describing his work,

I have been exploring the utility of the system as the major unit, focusing on political life as a system of behavior operating within and responding to its social environment as it makes binding allocations of values.[18]

The connection between general systems theory and input-output analysis, as elaborated by Easton, is therefore very substantial. But the input-output approach adopts specific positions on several of the unsettled issues of general systems theory, which should be noted at this point. Above all, Easton deals with "constructive" rather than *natural* systems as that distinction was laid out in Chapter Two. This means that "any set of variables selected for description and explanation"[19] constitutes a system at least for purposes of preliminary and basic research. At the same time this position necessitates the development of criteria to distinguish between interesting and trivial systems as research progresses. Although it is perfectly possible to discuss almost any set of variables in systemic terms, "all may not have equal utility for understanding political life."[20]

Another important distinction deals with the differences between *membership* (i.e., concrete) systems and *analytic* systems. In terms of social phenomena, membership systems are those whose basic components are human beings and that can therefore be thought of as collections of individuals. Analytic systems, on the other hand, are abstractions that focus

[18] David Easton, *A Framework for Political Analysis* (Englewood Cliffs, N.J.: Prentice-Hall, 1965), p. 21.
[19] *Ibid.*, p. 30.
[20] *Ibid.*, p. 36.

Systems Derivatives

on selected elements of human behavior. In this context we may distinguish a wide range of types of analytic system such as political, economic, or religious systems. Easton's argument is that relatively few membership systems are interesting for purposes of political analysis; analytic systems, however, are important focal points for research in political science as well as in a number of other disciplines.

The political system is therefore an analytic system existing within the over-all membership system formed by a society. In particular, the political system is "that system of interactions in any society through which binding or authoritative allocations are made and implemented."[21] The making of binding and authoritative decisions distinguishes the political system from other systems both within and outside the over-all society that form the environment of the political system. Easton also differentiates political and parapolitical systems in the following terms:

> I shall refer to internal political systems of groups and organizations as *parapolitical systems* and retain the concept "political system" for political life in the most inclusive unit being analyzed, namely, in society.[22]

Easton's own work focuses on the "political system," but it seems clear that the concepts and propositions of input-output analysis could be applied to parapolitical systems in many instances with equal success.

To continue, input-output analysis treats all political systems as both open and adaptive systems. In fact, the most salient focus of the approach is on the nature of the exchanges and transactions that take place between a political system and its environment. This has several important implications for analysis: It focuses attention on various concepts concerning systemic boundaries and boundary conditions; it brings up the concepts that lend their name to the approach by emphasizing that political systems perform work in processing and converting a variety of inputs into outputs; this in turn leads to a number of questions concerning systemic responsiveness that are of major importance throughout the development of the input-output approach. In short, political activities constitute "a system of behavior embedded in an environment to the influences of which the political system itself is exposed and in turn reacts."[23]

The conceptual structure of the input-output approach as elaborated by Easton centers around two sets of core variables. In the first place, throughout the whole presentation there is a very strong, underlying concern with questions relating to systemic persistence, sources of stress,

[21] *Ibid.*, p. 50.
[22] *Ibid.*, p. 52.
[23] David Easton, *A Systems Analysis of Political Life* (New York: Wiley, 1965), p. 18.

Systems Derivatives

and modes or processes of regulating stress. Easton poses his main question as follows:

How do any and all political systems manage to persist in a world of both stability and change? Ultimately the search for an answer will reveal what I have called the life process of political systems—those fundamental functions without which no system could endure—together with the typical modes of response through which systems manage to sustain them. The analysis of these processes, and of the nature and conditions of the responses, I posit as a central problem of political theory.[24]

The central position given to the concept of *persistence* raises a variety of additional points concerning the essential variables without which a political system could not exist and the critical ranges within which these variables can fluctuate. The whole notion of stress takes on meaning in terms of these concepts concerning persistence. "Stress will be said to occur when there is a danger that the essential variables will be pushed beyond what we may designate as their *critical range*."[25] A great deal of analysis in the input-output approach, therefore, deals with developments that may threaten to drive the essential variables of a political system beyond their critical ranges, and with the various regulatory responses to these developments which a system can make.

The second major sequence of concepts encompasses what Easton calls the *summary* variables. This sequence deals with inputs from various environments in the form of demands and supports, conversion processes, outputs, and feedback mechanisms that inject the effects and consequences of outputs back into a system as inputs. A political system is therefore not only a set of processes routinely converting inputs into outputs; it is a complex cyclical operation that has a dynamic of its own and that is capable of being purposive and goal-directed. Each segment of the operating cycle of a political system is susceptible to its own special types of stress and maintenance difficulties; but at the same time there are typical regulatory processes that go with each segment of the cycle and that serve to counterbalance stress problems. The bulk of the input-output approach deals with the analysis of the workings of political systems in terms of this second sequence of concepts followed by discussions of the common stress patterns and regulatory processes at each stage in the political cycle.

For purposes of analysis, the cycle of a political system can be broken into at virtually any point. In elaborating his input-output approach, however, Easton has chosen to begin with one of the major summary

24 *Ibid.*, p. 17.
25 *Ibid.*, p. 24.

Systems Derivatives

variables comprising inputs, namely, demands. "A demand may be defined as an expression of opinion that an authoritative allocation with regard to a particular subject matter should or should not be made by those responsible for doing so."[26] Demands go through a long conversion process before reaching the output stage in a political system, which trims down and formulates the great mass of initial demands in ways that make it possible for the political system to deal with them meaningfully. Starting even before the articulation of demands with a mass of conscious but undifferentiated wants, the cycle of a political system proceeds from the articulation of recognizable demands through the formulation of specific issues to the output of binding decisions. This conversion process is also a weeding out procedure. Though many demands are articulated, only a restricted number can reach the output stage while many more fall by the wayside at some stage in the conversion processes.

In conceptual terms there are several major types of stress inherent in the demand segment of the political cycle. If we view demands as message units calling for authoritative action, the whole problem of overload emerges as central to demand stress. Overload of this kind can stem either from excess quantities of demands (volume stress) or from some qualitative elements in the nature of particular demands (content stress). The phenomenon of stress in the demand segment of the cycle is also highly related to time factors. Given enough time, a political system can manage to handle a wide range of types and quantities of demands, but overload problems tend to take on great importance when available time is very restricted and quantitative levels of current demands are very high.

Briefly, there are four broad types of regulatory mechanisms commonly used in political systems for handling difficulties relating to want conversion and demand stress. Structural mechanisms focus on the phenomenon of *gatekeeping* at the boundary of the political system, which is designed to regulate the flow of wants entering the system and becoming articulated demands. All political systems develop gatekeeping roles and operating rules to be followed by gatekepers. Cultural mechanisms, on the other hand, encompass various sociocultural norms which, though usually *de facto* and tacit, establish influential criteria of appropriateness for the articulation of political demands. A third mode of demand regulation centers on developing adequate communications channels. The principal possibilities here include taking steps to increase the numbers and the capacities of relevant channels. Finally, demands can be regulated by various reduction processes during the conversion phases of the political cycle. Specific procedures included here are the collection and combination

[26] *Ibid.*, p. 38.

Systems Derivatives

of compatible demands, intrasystem gatekeeping procedures, and the requirement that general demands be converted into specific issues for purposes of political processing.

The other summary variable dealing with inputs is the concept of *support*. Supports refer to the remaining input transactions between a system and its environment after demands have been substracted. Easton defines support by saying that "A supports B either when A acts on behalf of B or when he orients himself favorably toward B. B may be a person or group; it may be a goal, idea, or institution."[27] In the course of the succeeding analysis a number of important distinctions appear which shed light on the undifferentiated notion of support. Overt support refers to actions that are clearly and manifestly supportive while covert support refers to supportive attitudes or sentiments. Moreover, it is necessary to differentiate between support directed toward each of three distinguishable political objects that are components of all political systems. These political objects include (1) the political community, which consists of the members of the system "seen as a group of persons bound together by a political division of labor,"[28] (2) the regime or basic values, political structure and norms, and (3) the political authorities who held power at any given time. Support for these objects will vary, at least in part, independently, even though there is likely to be a correlation between developments in each of these areas. Finally, it is virtually always necessary to speak in terms of balances of negative and positive supports. Since unanimity hardly ever occurs in political systems, concepts dealing with differences between positive and negative levels of support and the marginal production of support become relevant.

Just as in the case of demands, there are typical problems of support stress. As Easton puts it, persistence depends upon

. . . the maintenance of a minimal level of attachment for each of the three identified political objects. Where the input of support falls below this minimum, the persistence of any kind of system will be endangered.[29]

The decline or erosion of political support can occur for a number of reasons, but "a large part of them may be summed up under one category: output failure."[30] The point is that a system allocating values over time in ways that dissatisfy a substantial proportion of its members will gradually begin to lose the support that it formerly enjoyed. Easton's analysis also

[27] *Ibid.*, p. 159.
[28] *Ibid.*, p. 177.
[29] *Ibid.*, p. 220.
[30] *Ibid.*, p. 230.

Systems Derivatives

attaches central importance to the role of political cleavages and conflicts as major sources of support stress. It should also be noticed that so long as a system is basically sound, it can adapt to the erosion of support in some specific areas without necessarily encountering basic problems of stability.

Typical responses to support stress can be divided into several categories. Structural regulation refers to the possibility of reducing support stress by changing structural elements of the system. Examples include altering respresentational systems, patterns of groupings such as parties, or regime norms. Beyond such structural regulation a distinction must be made between diffuse support and specific support. Specific support encompasses support generated as a direct response to definable outputs of the system, while diffuse support covers various types of supportive actions and attitudes not directly related to specific outputs. Discussion here will focus on diffuse support since the more specific types of support are treated along with outputs. The generation of diffuse support is an important regulator of support stress since specific support is almost always inadequate by itself for the maintenance of a political system. Procedures for encouraging the development of diffuse support for a regime and its authorities center on the generation of a sense of legitimacy and of the feeling that there is a common or public interest furthered by the persistence of the political system. Building up diffuse support for the political system refers primarily to various processes for developing and spreading a sense of community among its members.[31]

The outputs of a political system are the authoritative decisions and actions of the system's leaders that bear on the allocation of values for the system. They are the results of conversion processes acting upon a great variety of demands and supports and can be conveniently divided into verbal statements and concrete performances. Just as in the case of the other summary variables, there are several important conceptual distinctions that elaborate on the undifferentiated notion of outputs. Outputs are the immediate or primary results of authoritative decisions, while the secondary and tertiary ramifications that occur over time are conceptualized as outcomes. Associated outputs are similar to authoritative outputs in form and function but they do not have the binding, compulsory nature of the latter.[32] They are, nevertheless, important in the alleviation of certain types of support stress. Moreover, outputs may be oriented in either an intrasystem or an extrasystem direction. This distinction hinges on the objects affected by the consequences of outputs.

Among other things outputs are an important type of response to

[31] For the distinction between political community and the *sense* of political community, see *ibid.*, Chapter 21.

[32] On the differences between these concepts, consult *ibid.*, pp. 354–362.

Systems Derivatives

support stress in a political system, and it is this aspect of outputs that is especially emphasized in Easton's approach. As he himself puts it, outputs

. . . may help to maintain a minimal level of support for the various political objects. It is this aspect of outputs that tends to be neglected in theoretical inquiry and which lies at the heart of this part of our analysis.[33]

In this connection, outputs are primarily a means of generating specific support, though over a period of time a satisfactory flow of outputs may also result in increases in various types of diffuse support.

It is possible for outputs to play a crucial role in generating specific support for a political system because of the existence of feedback loops that complete the cycle of a political system and that make it a dynamic and regenerative operation. Although there are many feedback processes that go on within a political system, the input-output approach focuses primarily on the over-all systemic feedback loop that links the consequences of outputs with the continuing inflow of inputs. Feedback is essentially a dynamic process through which information about the performance of a system is communicated in such a way as to effect the subsequent behavior of the system. For the purposes of input-output analysis, feedback can be broken down into negative feedback, which deals with error regulation, and into goal-changing feedback, which deals with problems of purposive redirection. Thus feedback is essentially a regulative element in a political system, though it is subject to various pathologies itself as regards such matters as accuracy, responsiveness, and time lags.

The input-output approach distinguishes four segments of the systemic feedback loop that are especially relevant from the point of view of maintaining or increasing specific support. Feedback stimuli stem from authoritative or associated outputs and outcomes and provide a substantial part of the environment to which the system itself reacts. Since reactions are ultimately by individual human beings, problems of perception and perceived feedback stimuli as well as questions concerning *circumstantial* feedback stimuli become very important.[34] Feedback response forms the second segment of the feedback loop, which is concerned primarily with levels of demand satisfaction and the generation of negative and positive support. Following this segment is a set of questions dealing with the communication of feedback responses to the authorities in a political system. Central concepts refer to accuracy, distortion, and various types of delay in the communication of feedback responses. Finally, the cycle is completed and starts over with the discussion of output reaction to

[33] *Ibid.*, p. 347.
[34] For the differences between circumstantial and perceived feedback stimuli, see *ibid.*, pp. 383–391.

Systems Derivatives

feedback on the part of the authorities. Relevant variables here focus on the responsiveness of the authorities, output lags, and the resources available to the authorities to make decisions in response to informational feedback. The analysis of feedback processes completes the logical progression set up both by the sequence of variables dealing with persistence, stress, and regulation and by the sequence of variables focusing on inputs and outputs.

It is interesting to note that input-output analysis in its present form is somewhat at variance with the general position concerning approaches to analysis which Easton expressed in his earlier work some years ago. In terms of the distinctions set forth in Chapter One, input-output analysis seems to fall closest to the position associated with Almond. It consists primarily of a detailed framework of concepts, though a number of hypotheses and propositions are brought in at various stages. And the interesting thing about the hypotheses and propositions is that they rest on a combination of deductively derived material and generally accepted empirical material. Thus Easton describes the approach as "a conceptual framework around which the more complex structure of a theory may possibly, in the slowness of time, be added."[35]

Several points concerning the functions of input-output analysis and the areas in which the approach seems most useful are in order. To begin with, the approach is at its strongest in dealing with the kinds of questions discussed in this volume under the heading of system maintenance. Here the conceptual richness of the approach goes substantially beyond the more usual and somewhat static analyses of stability and equilibrium and focuses on concepts such as disturbance, stress, regulation and purposive redirection, all of which lends a significant dynamism to the analysis of system maintenance. And in fact, it is necessary to call attention at this point to the utility of input-output analysis in dealing with questions concerning change and dynamics. Easton is essentially correct in arguing that

> The idea of systems persistence extends far beyond that of systems maintenance; it is oriented toward exploring change as well as stability, both of which may be interpreted as alternative avenues for coping with stress.[36]

There are several types of change given major attention in input-output analysis. Above all, the political system is seen as a conversion process performing work, producing outputs, and altering its environment, with a continuous exchange between a political system and its environments based on the steady operation of dynamic processes. At the same time the

[35] *Ibid.*, p. 12.
[36] Easton, *A Framework, op. cit.*, p. 88.

Systems Derivatives

approach provides numerous concepts for dealing both with political dynamics in the form of systemic adaptation processes and even with purposive redirection in the form of goal-changing feedback. With this perspective it is possible to deal with changes in the system itself, although the approach focuses mainly on changes whose principal results are only to modify or streamline the system. It is therefore important to observe that the input-output approach does not dwell extensively on a third level of change and dynamics focusing on broader-scale and more far-reaching alterations. Revolutionary change is hardly mentioned and even the possibilities of evolution to new systemic forms are not covered in detail. Though the adaptive consequences of phenomena like growth could certainly be treated under this approach, their broader aspects of qualitative change do not find much place therein.

In its present form input-output analysis contains a somewhat uneven coverage of the area of political goals and goal-attainment. It puts, of course, great emphasis on questions concerning systemic persistence, and the various processes for attaining this goal are dealt with at length and in detail. The goal of persistence, however, is very much bound up with problems of systemic survival and the preservation of essential variables within their critical ranges. For this reason, the analysis of goal-attainment in this restricted sense belongs more to the study of system maintenance than to the analysis of more nearly teleological questions concerning values, end states, and the instrumental processes of attaining them. The approach contains comparatively little material concerning goals and values beyond the question of persistence. There is the general proposition that political systems do work, and it is understood that they can be operated with various goals in mind, but the approach is not rich in conceptual materials for the analysis of these questions.

As is the case with any approach, there are various types of question that input-output analysis does not emphasize and that are simply not handled in detail by its conceptual apparatus. Several examples should suffice to make this point explicit. Various questions concerning patterns of control, power, and influence do not play an important part in input-output analysis. Most of the systemic approaches share this pattern of deemphasis to some extent since they focus on the operation of a system in fairly abstract terms rather than on the behavior patterns of human beings. To continue, input-output analysis has little to say about the politics of decline, disruption, and breakdown in political systems. The material on change that is included does not, for the most part, address itself to the more abrupt and pathological kinds of change under these headings. Easton himself admits that he is far more impressed with the self-maintaining capacities of political systems than with the phenomena of political decay and degeneration. And although some of the concepts in the approach could conceivably be turned toward analysis in this area, there is little scope for such analysis in the approach in its present form. A final example deals with the fact that input-output analysis is not particularly well suited for the analysis of mass political phenomena such as voting, political attitude formation, followership, and so forth. Throughout the conceptual material of the approach care is frequently taken to restrict the application of concepts and hypotheses to the politically relevant members of the system. Although the notion of political relevancy is not precisely delimited, it is clear that it does not include mass phenomena.

There are several features of input-output analysis that make it attractive for comparative analysis: not only does it present a nicely standardized set of concepts and categories that have the advantage of being logically inclusive, it is also pitched at a level that facilitates the piecing together of broad and comparable overviews of whole political systems, a characteristic that is highly desirable at present since the discipline is not yet very well prepared for detailed comparative work on many secondary and subsidiary questions. Moreover, the approach is deliberately formulated at such a level of abstraction that it avoids the dangers of becoming tied to any particular type of political system or to any specific variety of sociocultural context. This procedure, of course, sometimes carries with it the danger of loss of content due to high levels of abstraction, but the importance of avoiding biases toward certain types of systems is crucial in comparative analysis.

Before turning to some of the criticisms that can be leveled at input-output analysis, we should note briefly that it is undoubtedly the most inclusive systemic approach so far constructed specifically for political analysis by a political scientist. As mentioned earlier, the various systemic approaches have more typically been adapted from other disciplines for use in political analysis. This gives input-output analysis a distinct advantage since it is able to deal with the various problems of applying systems analysis to political questions in a coordinated fashion without having to cope with the problems of adaptation.

One of the problems in constructing a critique of input-output analysis stems from the fact that the approach has not yet been applied extensively and in detail in empirical political research. It is to be expected that some of its advantages and disadvantages will show up more clearly with the growth of a body of applications. There are, nevertheless, a number of points that can be made at this time by way of a critique.

Above all, there are several senses in which the input-output approach does not constitute the general or unified theory of politics for which Easton seemed to have hoped in his earlier work. First, it is not necessarily

46

accurate in either a logical or an empirical sense that questions concerning systems persistence constitute the most inclusive questions for political analysis. Easton maintains that

> Persistence and change of systems, or rather, persistence through change has seemed to be the most inclusive kind of question that one might ask about a political system.[37]

Although questions concerning persistence are undoubtedly important, there is no definitive reason to classify them as somehow more basic than questions concerning patterns of control and, especially, goals and goal attainment. Second, the fact that the input-output approach tends to focus in a *de facto* sense on *national* political systems leads to a relative deemphasis of many phenomena that are normally classified as political. This is true to some extent in the analysis of the specific workings or intra-system processes and mechanisms of individual political systems. But the point is even more clear-cut in relation to the relative lack of emphasis on interactions among political systems or the phenomena that are normally classified as international relations.

A somewhat related problem stems from the fact that focusing on questions concerning persistence and stress at the level of the over-all unit or political system downgrades the attention that is devoted to concrete allocative or distributive questions concerning who gets what.[38] This point ties in both with the lack of emphasis in input-output analysis on many areas of goal attainment and with the fact that the approach tends to deal with systemic processes and functions at the expense of any real emphasis on specific human behavior patterns. Since the political system is a consciously analytic construct in input-output analysis, roles and patterns of roles are much more nearly the basic unit of analysis than individuals and groups of individuals. And even in the discussion of roles, the flow of analysis is directed toward the contribution of various role patterns to the persistence of the system, rather than toward the contribution of the system to the well-being of the role holders. As a result the approach deals extensively with the systemic consequences of political decisions, but it tends to reduce opportunities for the analysis of concrete decision-making processes and of the allocative as opposed to the systemic consequences of decisions. This is by no means to argue that focusing on systemic perspectives is bad or faulty; quite the contrary, such a focus is often very fruitful. The point is that a systemic focus does not result in a general "theory" of

---

[37] Easton, *A Systems Analysis, op. cit.*, p. 475.
[38] For indications that Easton is at least to some extent aware of this problem see *ibid.*, Chapter 29.

47

politics since it leaves out various important questions; it is well to keep this in mind in pursuing empirical research.

Although it is difficult to tell how practice will work out, it seems likely that input-output analysis in its present form contains something of an elitist orientation. Throughout the conceptual framework the central focus is on the politically relevant members. Though this concept is not defined in precise operational terms, such a focus is very likely to lead to a concentration on various elite groups and elite roles in the course of actual empirical research. This consequence is not intrinsically bad, but it is important to remember that the results will again be a departure from a general "theory" of politics and a relative neglect of various politically relevant phenomena. Several examples of the types of phenomena that will probably be deemphasized for this reason were cited above in the discussion of the functions of input-output analysis for political science.

It is also probable that the input-output approach will be charged from time to time with harboring a *status quo* bias. The problem here is somewhat similar to the one discussed earlier in connection with structural-functional analysis, i.e., whenever an approach attaches central importance to questions concerning persistence, adaptation, and the regulation of stress, it becomes liable to charges of this kind. In the case of input-output analysis it is true that the approach places relatively little emphasis on matters concerning revolutionary or large-scale change; on the contrary, the emphasis is on functional and modifying processes of change. There are, however, several points that should be made in response to such criticisms. To begin with, input-output analysis does not pretend to justify *status quo* conditions in any normative sense. It is simply a framework for organizing, conceptualizing, codifying, and manipulating data. But beyond this, there is probably even less specific substance to this charge in regard to input-output analysis than there is in the case of structural-functional analysis, since the former has a more substantial conceptual basis for the analysis of dynamic processes. The emphasis on such dynamic processes as the purposive redirection of goals, for example, argues against the charge that input-output analysis is excessively *status quo* oriented.

Finally, there are several minor problems that can be grouped together under the heading of procedural criticisms. The approach occasionally falls prey to the dangers of rationalism and the forcing of logical neatness onto politics, even though the level of awareness of these problems is commendable in most instances. Moreover, the characteristic deductivism of work of this kind sometimes leads to formulas that would be very difficult to operationalize in practice. And the approach is not entirely free of distortions of common usage that are likely to cause a certain amount of confusion for practitioners.

48

Systems Derivatives

Approaches from Communications Theory and Cybernetics

In line with the general propensity of political
scientists to borrow perspectives and frames of reference
from other disciplines, a number of analysts have been working
in recent years on an approach to analysis that leans
heavily on the basic orientations of communications theory
and cybernetics. Both of these areas represent
relatively young and fast-moving developments
in scientific analysis, having received a great impetus
from the Second World War

and from the speed of the subsequent revolution in technology. The dynamism and rapid advance of these theoretical constructs have, no doubt, made them particularly attractive to analysts in other disciplines. Amongst political scientists, by far the most important and salient example of an approach to analysis using cybernetics and communications theory is to be found in the work of Karl Deutsch. Though he has not yet elaborated an inclusive or definitive approach, he has made an impressive start in this direction and appears to be moving toward the development of a full-scale approach. For these reasons the present discussion focuses particularly on the work of Deutsch.

The Nature of the Approach

At the outset we shall state several important points of general orientation that flow from an approach emphasizing cybernetics and communications theory. Most importantly, politics and government appear in essence as processes of *steering* and *coordinating* human efforts toward the attainment of some set of goals.[1] Within this framework the basic mechanism through which these processes manifest themselves is the *decision*. It is important to note specifically, however, that this approach devotes particular attention to the processes of *making* decisions as contrasted with the actual *consequences* of decisions. It is a legacy of its background in cybernetics and communications theory that the approach focuses on decision making as *process* rather than on the results of decisions.

Several additional points of orientation stem from this posture. First, the approach emphasizes at all points problems of dynamics and of the various information flows attendant upon communications and decision making. Second, the information flow therefore constitutes the basic unit of analysis. But a flow of this kind can be seen in turn as being comprised of two elements. The actual flow arises from the movement of bits of information through the relevant system. In addition, however, there are various structures that shape this flow of information with important consequences for the resultant decisions.

Though interest in models is presently high among political scientists, this approach places a particularly strong emphasis on working models of the type that one thinks of in connection with engineering. There are at least two major reasons for this: (1) the emphasis on processes and flows rather than on distribution or allocation leads naturally to an interest in constructing replicas of the basic dynamics of the operation; (2) the approach stems from several bodies of theory that have long been associated

[1] Karl W. Deutsch, *The Nerves of Government* (Glencoe, Ill.: The Free Press, 1963), p. 124.

Approaches from Communications Theory and Cybernetics

with the construction of working models. In his work in this area Deutsch has offered several models of some interest. One central model is fundamental to his entire approach, however, and that is a model which offers a graphic presentation of government as a decision-making system based on various information flows. Though Deutsch has presented an elaborate picture of this basic model, we have simplified it to illustrate its essentials.[2]

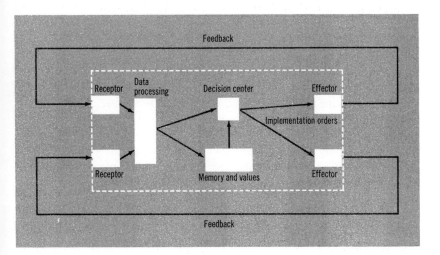

Consideration of this model offers a good format for a brief description of the principal concepts that Deutsch's approach employs in the analysis of government and politics. These concepts fall into several distinct categories, the first of which deals with important concepts relating to operating structures. The various receptors or reception systems deal with the intake of information from domestic and foreign (or external) environments. The notion of reception actually covers several functions beyond simple intake, including scanning operations, selection of information, and data processing. Most systems develop a set of fairly specific operating rules for processing the flow of incoming information. Within the decision-making apparatus, information is handled and acted upon by structures representing memory, value complexes, and actual decision centers. Memory relates incoming information to relevant past experiences concerning both processes and consequences, while values perform the normative task of relating possibilities to preferences. Finally, there are structures that

[2] This figure is drawn from Deutsch's far more complex presentation. See *ibid.*, p. 258.

Approaches from Communications Theory and Cybernetics

operate to implement completed decisions and to feed information concerning performances back into the apparatus as a new input.

A second category of concepts focuses on various flows and processes, and the central notion in this area is a patterned set of information flows that together form a communications network. Important concepts in analyzing the communications networks of political systems deal with channels, loads, and load capacity. Load capacity is a function of the number and types of available channels, while *load* itself relates to the over-all intake of information at any given time. One should note that in political systems loads tend to vary substantially over time as well as to differ significantly in qualitative characteristics. In addition, load capacity is closely related to factors concerning responsiveness, fidelity, background noise, and distortion. Responsiveness refers to the facility of the apparatus in taking account of and handling incoming information. The notion of fidelity, on the other hand, refers to the accuracy with which information is transmitted in the various processes of perception, selection, and handling. Important variables affecting the level of fidelity include various types of specific distortions as well as the general background noise that tends to obscure relevant information. A further process concept centers on the notion of recall—the ability of the communications system to associate, locate, and bring forth past experience that is relevant to the analysis of incoming information. All of these process elements combine to determine the *combinatorial capacity* of the over-all operation. Combinatorial capacity is a measure of ability to deal with a wide range of information inputs in such a way as to make and implement decisions with positive consequences for the attainment of the goals of a political system.

This leads to a third category of concepts that deal with the results or consequences of the various decision processes. Though outcomes receive less emphasis than processes in this approach, it is necessary at least to state the nature of the outcomes. In the first instance outcomes take the form of decisions which constitute a flow of prescriptions to be effected. This raises several additional points that require conceptualization. In order to assess the results of a flow of decisions, one must be able to state the goals or purposes toward which the decisions aim. Since the approach is not strongly oriented toward analyzing the processes through which goals are set, it tends to deal with this problem in the language of teleology. Beyond this, the question of outcomes raises several considerations concerning compliance, effectiveness, and authority. The consequences of a flow of decisions for the attainment of various goals will depend in considerable part on the extent to which decisions are complied with and achieve effective implementation. At this point, the general concepts of control and steering begin to come more clearly into focus.

Approaches from Communications Theory and Cybernetics

What means can a decision-making system employ to regulate its actions so that they will maximize the extent to which relevant goals are achieved? In the work of Deutsch one major response to this question focuses on the analysis of feedback and feedback processes. From the point of view of regulatory operations, negative feedback is the center of attention. Negative feedback refers to the processes through which information about the consequences of decisions and implementing actions is put back into a system in such a way as to alter the system's behavior in directions that will lead closer to the attainment of relevant goals. This is what happens, for example, when a thermostat reacts to a rise in temperature by shutting off a furnace and to a subsequent fall in temperature by turning it on again. The operation of negative feedback processes assumes the existence of definable goals and purposes; and as such it constitutes a crucial form of regulatory control.

There are several more specific concepts that are central to an explanation of the workings of negative feedback, including load, lag, gain, and lead.[3] *Load* refers to the extensiveness of a system's activities relative to available feedback facilities and to the quantities of information involved in feedback processes relative to channel capacities. *Lag* is a measure of delay in reporting and acting on information about the consequences of decisions and actions, whereas *gain* represents the extensiveness of a system's responses to this information following its receipt. *Lead,* on the other hand, is the ability to act in response to forecasts of future consequences, as is the case when one aims ahead of a moving object in order to hit it. The interactions of these variables determine the consequences of the feedback processes. As Deutsch states it, "The chances of success in goal seeking are always inversely related to the amounts of *load* and *lag.* Up to a point they may be positively related to the amounts of *gain,* although at high rates of gain this relationship may be reversed; and they are always positively related to the amount of *lead.*"[4] It is possible to measure the efficiency of a negative feedback process "in terms of the number and size of its mistakes, that is the under- and over-corrections it makes in reaching the goal."[5]

Control operations based on negative feedback are subject to a variety of pathologies and disruptions. The flow of feedback information may lack fidelity or it may be subject to distortions of selectivity that are seriously dysfunctional. There are also the possibilities that a decision-making system will tend to drift without adequate goals or be insufficiently responsive to feedback information at the point of reception. Perhaps the most important

3 *Ibid.,* pp. 187–190.
4 *Ibid.,* pp. 188–189.
5 *Ibid.,* p. 187.

Approaches from Communications Theory and Cybernetics

feedback pathology occurs, however, when positive or amplifying feedback processes replace negative feedback. Positive feedback occurs when information fed back into the system catalyzes only actions that constitute an increment to or are augmentation of the original action. The result is not a regulatory process but an upward spiral of responses. This is the fundamental basis of many security dilemmas among individuals, cycles, or swings in economic exchanges, and arms races among nations. Important variables in gauging positive feedback processes deal with the nature of responses or reactions and with fuel supplies. Successively smaller responses at each round of the spiral will have a dampening effect, while overreactions will lead in the opposite direction. In addition, the potential scope of a positive feedback process will be determined by available fuel, as is the case, for example, with forest fires or qualitative arms races based on advances in technology. It is important to emphasize, however, that positive feedback processes are sometimes capable of inducing breakdown or radical change in decision-making systems.

Although the emphasis on feedback processes is clear, Deutsch's general interest in the control of political systems has led him to broaden his perspectives to cover material concerning homeostasis and cybernetics. Homeostasis refers quite generally to all processes of self-regulation and allows for various possibilities of dynamic change and adaptation, as well as static replication of a single operation. Such an expansion of scope is of obvious importance in dealing with processes of politics and government. The term cybernetics is even more general since it has come to refer to all processes of steering and control in various types of systems. The immediate relevance of this broadened perspective stems from the fact that there are steering pathologies in decision-making systems that are not covered in the analysis of feedback. These problems include (1) the degradation of data processing operations or the loss of coordination of elements in internal decision-making processes; (2) the loss of depth of memory; and (3) the inability to adapt to changing environmental conditions relating, for example, to technology or the nature of external systems.

Beyond this, however, a broadened perspective is crucial in distinguishing the whole area of change from that of repetitive processes. Deutsch argues strongly in favor of focusing on the concept of stability, which is characteristic of discussions of feedback and homeostasis, as compared with the analysis of *equilibrium*.[6] He criticizes what he calls the *equilibrium approach* as being both mechanistic and excessively detached from the impact of environmental factors. Even more basic, however, is his argument that the equilibrium approach is not adequate to handle directional movement along a path through time. Equilibrium is characteristic

[6] *Ibid.*, pp. 88–91.

Approaches from Communications Theory and Cybernetics

of unchanging systems that essentially repeat the same process time after time. Politics and government, however, differ from such systems on two counts: first, they perform work and accomplish objectives in such a way as to change their basic positions vis-à-vis their environments; second, they have at least some ability to change themselves in the course of steering toward various goals. In this connection, an analysis of stability and particularly of stability in the context of a dynamic operation is necessary. This is an important step in moving from the discussion of mechanistic communications systems to dynamic political systems.

Questions concerning adaptation and directional change occupy an important position in the Deutschian approach to political analysis. Although political processes are less susceptible to externally imposed alterations than most inanimate systems, they do not generally break down, and they frequently demonstrate substantial adaptive capacities of their own. Drawing on the broader perspectives outlined above, Deutsch has significantly extended his basic conceptions concerning communications and decision-making to address these problems of political analysis. Such extensions are among his most creative contributions to political analysis.

To begin with, there are the concepts of goal-changing feedback and learning in the context of political operations. Political systems sometimes face situations in which their original goals are either largely fulfilled or become increasingly difficult to attain. Goal-changing feedback refers to the intake of information concerning such developments in a form that facilitates appropriate alterations of goals on the part of a system. Learning is, then, the ability of the political operation to adapt its modes of action in response to such information. This can actually be accomplished through the recombination of elements of internal structure and process in appropriate ways. This approach also emphasizes learning *capacity* as well as actual learning. The capacity to learn refers to the availability of elements for recombination, as distinguished from the actual processes of recombination. It is therefore a measure of the flexibility or rigidity of a political operation. It is through these processes that political systems adapt both to changes in their environments and to changes that follow as a consequence of their own actions.

More basically, there are also the processes of self-transformation that focus on such notions as innovation and growth. A political operation must move beyond mere adaptation to changes if it is (1) to avoid stagnation and long-term decline, and (2) to grow. The notions in the previous paragraph refer to adaptive changes in goals, structures, or processes. Here the question concerns changes that are so fundamental and far-reaching as to induce qualitative transformations in a political operation over time. It is clear that environmental changes can sometimes impose transformations or

Approaches from Communications Theory and Cybernetics

even breakdown on a system from outside its confines. Self-transformation, however, refers to an ability to generate self-sustaining processes of change internally and in so doing ultimately to produce qualitative changes over time. A system with a capability of this kind could actually replace itself, a result that is far more common in social systems than in inanimate communications systems.

Functions of the Approach

As stated earlier the approach to political analysis stemming from communications theory and cybernetics has not as yet been fully worked out. It is, however, already possible to discuss the functions of the approach especially in connection with the relatively advanced work of Deutsch. The approach goes considerably beyond the simple presentation of a set of concepts, classificatory categories, and criteria of relevance. The definitional system is a rather formal one, and Deutsch has added a number of hypotheses and propositions to this basic structure. The resultant material is of two types. First, there are a good many largely deductive propositions that rest squarely on the underlying principles and assumptions of communications theory and cybernetics. The main operations in this connection consist of efforts to point out applications to relevant political phenomena and to make the necessary adaptations. Second, especially as he begins to make extensions of the basic conceptions of communications theory, Deutsch elaborates additional hypotheses relevant to political analysis by (1) introducing a number of empirically based generalizations, and (2) reasoning back and forth between his basic model and examples of actual political phenomena.

The approach as set forth by Deutsch generates a powerful thrust toward the effort to operationalize hypotheses and to engage in quantitative analysis. This thrust stems at least partly from the origins of the approach in the rather operational work of communications theory and cybernetics. In addition, it is certainly related to the emphasis of the approach on decision-making as a process rather than on the results or consequences of decisions. As a result the approach tends to focus on *flows* of information and on the forms of various structures rather than on the substance of either. By way of example, the Deutschian approach leads to an interest in quantities of trade, size of mail flows, and numbers of diplomatic agreements. Variables of this kind are far more susceptible to quantitative treatment than those emphasized by some of the other approaches.

In discussing the functions of this approach it is important to reiterate that all approaches are by nature selective; even in areas where a given approach is strong there is no implication that it can take the place of other

56

approaches utilizing divergent modes of conceptualization. In the antecedent area of description, the approach from communications theory and cybernetics is rich and extensive. It also has the advantage of focusing sharply on certain variables and of treating them in terms of concepts that are relatively new to political analysis. It is necessary, however, to pay something for these gains. Deutsch's categories are at times somewhat rigid when applied to the fluidity of politics. This is a legacy of their origin in the analysis of more precise and concrete operations. Moreover, the approach sometimes treats well-known political phenomena in terms far from common sense or lexically accepted meanings. While this is a real problem, it is ultimately excusable in cases where the use of the approach leads to constructive insights.

The broad area of power and control presents some difficulties for the Deutschian approach. The previous section stressed the pervasive interest of this approach in the problems of control and the processes of steering and coordination. These questions become, in fact, the subject of a number of hypotheses and propositions. The problem in this instance, however, arises from the fact that this posture generates a conception of political power somewhat limited in its coverage. Though the translation is a little awkward, one can discuss the location of power and many of the techniques of utilizing it in terms of a conception based on the flow of information through various structures. But other important questions concerning power are harder to handle in these terms. Such questions include (1) varying degrees of power in terms of scope and depth, (2) differences between power and influence, (3) the selection and behavior of various elites specializing in power, and (4) the sources of personal power. Unfortunately these are important questions in the analysis of political behavior and ones that can hardly be neglected in a good deal of political analysis.

As regards the area of pattern maintenance, the approach offers a number of guidelines. Though these problems are treated somewhat narrowly, they are handled in considerable depth. The substitution of the concept of stability in the face of dynamic developments for older notions of equilibrium is clearly useful. Moreover, the processes of coordination and regulation through feedback mechanisms receive very extensive treatment and give rise to a large number of propositions. The efficacy of various feedback mechanisms in dealing with certain steering pathologies is clearly of considerable importance. The broadening of perspectives to the more general consideration of homeostasis and cybernetics, however, has not yet produced as much material on problems of pattern maintenance as might be desired. In particular, there are some essentially internal decision-making and control pathologies that require considerably more con-

Approaches from Communications Theory and Cybernetics

ceptual attention than they receive at the present stage of development of this approach.

The approach from communications theory and cybernetics deals quite explicitly with various processes and dynamic movements so that it is quite well equipped to handle questions concerning change, as compared with other approaches currently in use in political analysis. Problems of "modificatory" change are incorporated closely into the approach since it is based on notions of dynamic processes that accomplish objectives and therefore alter the situation of the decision-making operation. The various concepts of learning and goal-changing feedback become important in this context. The approach is also attuned to problems of evolutionary change, a fact which gives it real advantages in some areas of political analysis. Self-transformation, innovation, and growth are given explicit treatment. Decision-making operations are likely to transform themselves completely over time in response to their own activities and to environmental changes, and this is an important perspective in the analysis of many political processes.

When it comes to the problems of revolutionary change and disruption, however, this approach, like many others in use today, is not particularly helpful. It does consider certain externally imposed difficulties, such as overload, as well as various internal problems like steering pathologies and amplifying feedback. Possibilities of revolutionary change are therefore not wholly neglected. Nevertheless, the approach focuses primarily on the problems of keeping systems going and on the various processes of adaptation that can be utilized to meet destabilizing forces. On the whole, the more revolutionary possibilities are most frequently lumped under the heading of breakdown and treated in terms of relevant avoidance mechanisms. This is unfortunate since the present period is one in which a number of political systems are facing the prospect of revolutionary breakdown and in which there are some indications that the over-all international system may be "actively" unstable. In such an environment, the processes of revolutionary change and the ways in which they can be controlled are of substantial interest.

Finally, the approach assumes a rather incomplete position with regard to the various problems of goal attainment. The general notion of goal attainment is given a rather prominent place since it is necessary for the analysis of purposeful decision-making as well as for the accomplishment of meaningful tasks in the operation of political processes. Deutsch quite rightly emphasizes that there can be no negative feedback processes without goals and purposes, and he is interested in operationalizing and ranking various objectives in order to facilitate analysis. At the same time, the approach tends to treat goal attainment simply as the end of a process and to concentrate on the various operations leading toward that end. For this reason it does not pay much attention to a number of problems of great concern to many political analysts. The processes by which goals are set and related to one another, for example, are not treated extensively except in the rather limited context of goal-changing feedback. Moreover, the various problems surrounding the allocation and distribution of values by means of political processes are frequently deemphasized. The fact that Deutsch tends to discuss goals in teleological terms is indicative of a relative lack of interest in the intricate processes of goal setting and in the normative problems of rationalizing value systems.

Toward a Critique

The approach from communications theory and cybernetics raises a number of problems, some of which are considerably more hampering than others. In this connection, it is relevant to reiterate a point made earlier, that any given approach harbors problems and pitfalls that, though actually avoidable, trap many of its practitioners.

The approach is quite frequently criticized for being mechanistic and for elaborating an essentially engineering orientation toward human behavior. Deutsch himself is clearly aware of this criticism and has constructed a defense against attack from this quarter. The key to his defense is the proposition that the simple dichotomy between mechanical and organic constructs is increasingly breaking down and becoming obsolete. In his view, rapidly advancing sophistication in dealing with machines, computers, and cybernetics in general is making this distinction less and less clear-cut. As he himself has stated,

> . . . the new experiences and notions promise to replace the classic analogues or models of mechanism, organism, and process, which so long have dominated so much of scientific thinking. All three of these models have long been felt inadequate.
>
> In the place of these obsolescent models, we now have an array of self-controlling machines that react to their environment, as well as to the results of their own behavior; that store, process, and apply information; and that have, in some cases, a limited capacity to learn.[7]

All of this does answer some of the criticisms of the approach to the effect that its constructs are static and therefore inadequate for dealing with dynamics or growth. It does not, however, satisfy the criticism which suggests that models of inanimate processes are somewhat inadequate as analogues to human behavior. The Deutschian approach still presents

[7] *Ibid.*, pp. 79–80.

problems along these lines. It offers a model that seems far more manipulable than most actual political operations; it often seems to discount irrational, fortuitous, or random behavior, and above all, it does not deal adequately with the nuances of human thought processes, the psychological consequences of world views and value systems, the subtleties of political leadership, and the nebulous quality of many political relations.

Certain problems significant for this approach stem from its emphasis on processes and its relative lack of concern with various consequences (or outcomes). It is quite clear, of course, that processes are important and worthy of analysis. The imbalance of focus between processes and outcomes, however, leads to certain biases having important consequences. Above all, there is a strong tendency to conceptualize political behavior largely in terms of performance indicators and subsequently to spell out these indicators in terms of flows of information, communications, or decisions. The almost inevitable consequence of this posture is a strong emphasis on the quantitative measurement of flows, as contrasted with an analysis of the quality of individual units and the substantive problems of politics. One common result is a tendency to obscure questions concerning basic political functions with a welter of material on flows and processes. Beyond this, however, quality may be of equal or greater importance than quantity in many political relationships.[8] To take a relevant example, the content of specific communications between two actors in a political system is frequently of equal or greater importance to the future of their relationship than the sheer volume of transactions between them.

An especially important derivative problem deals with the dangers of false counting and distorted quantification in the search for performance indicators. It would be foolish to downgrade the importance of political processes and of quantitative measurements. The work of practitioners of this approach, however, sometimes shows the opposite propensity. The quantity of mail flows, for example, conceals the nature of their content, and the sheer number of diplomatic agreements concluded between two countries may be very deceptive. Similarly, quantitative content analysis of the various flows of political information has a tendency to conceal the qualitative and contextual significance of what has been communicated. Some of the larger analytic operations catalyzed by Deutsch himself manifest problems of this kind. Many of the recent exercises focusing on the construction of data inventories, the expansion of mapping operations, and the proliferation of performance indicators, for example, are hampered

[8] For criticisms along this line, see Hedley Bull, "International Theory, the Case for a Classical Approach," *World Politics,* Vol. XVIII, No. 3 (April 1966), pp. 361–377.

Approaches from Communications Theory and Cybernetics

by the typical problems associated with the manipulation of data in search of a rationale.[9] Nevertheless, these pitfalls are not made inevitable by the decision to utilize the approach from communications theory and cybernetics. Though they are important, an analyst who is aware of their dimensions can skirt them to a considerable degree.

A third broad area of criticism deals with the problems of reasoning by analogy and of model building. Certain difficulties with analogies are of course inevitable in any approach that borrows heavily from other disciplines, and in this particular case several difficulties deserve specific mention. Most importantly, there is a problem that is almost the reverse of some of the commonly cited organismic difficulties. Here the chain of reasoning extends from concepts developed in an inanimate arena and referring specifically to machines to the analysis of political operations based very much on individuals and combinations of individuals. This point ties in with the problems noted above that stem from the underlying mechanistic propensities of the approach. In addition, analogic reasoning sometimes leads Deutsch to reify political processes and structures. What are actually nebulous operations with unclear boundaries occasionally appear as clear-cut, neat compartments of the basic model.

Model building is at present a very controversial subject among political scientists. The basic rationale of a model stems from its utility in simplifying a real situation that is too complex to analyze systematically, and Deutsch himself states this proposition clearly in a lengthy discussion of models.[10] In his own system, however, the model ultimately becomes so complex that it tends to move away from being a working model and toward becoming a schema. Though the core elements of the model are not unduly complex, great problems arise when Deutsch begins to expand the structure to deal with the nuances of political reality. What could remain a working model in the essentially operational field of communications becomes considerably more diffuse when applied to the more nebulous variables of political behavior. In short, the effort to shift models from one discipline to another tends to raise difficult problems.[11]

A final set of criticisms of the approach focuses on those problems that stem from the built-in logic of the basic communications perspective. Almost all approaches contain a kind of logic of their own sufficiently strong and pervasive to lead to various analytic biases. Several specific

[9] The work of the Yale Political Data Program, whose creation Deutsch inspired, offers some examples. See especially Bruce Russett and Hayward Alker, Karl Deutsch, and Harold Lasswell, *World Handbook of Political and Social Indicators* (New Haven: Yale University Press, 1964).

[10] Deutsch, *op. cit.*, Chapters 1–3.

[11] On this subject consult Martin Landau, "Due Process of Inquiry," *The American Behavioral Scientist*, Vol. IX, No. 2 (October 1965), pp. 4–10.

Approaches from Communications Theory and Cybernetics

factors of this kind deserve mention at this point. An earlier section pointed to the role of the basic communications perspectives in forcing departures from common sense and lexical meanings in a number of cases. In addition, on the level of structure the extensions required to allow the approach to deal with various problems of political change, transformation, and growth have a somewhat discontinuous quality. It is quite true that these extensions attest to the creative abilities of Deutsch, but they do not always mesh perfectly with the preceding engineering constructs drawn primarily from the analysis of inanimate systems.

Moreover, the logic of the approach results in several more substantive problems. First, resultant analyses sometimes manifest the qualities of formalism and excessive rationalism. Real decision-making procedures in political life often bear more resemblance to the notions of *incrementalism*[12] than to the formal processes of the Deutschian system. Second, the approach demands a higher degree of role specificity, formality of information channels and structures, settled processing procedures, and goal orientation than is visible in many important political processes of the real world. The basic thrust of these problems relates again to the fact that the shift from inanimate processes to human organizations involves significant discontinuities. In the end, therefore, this critique returns to the divergences between men and machines with which it started.

A Note on Snyder, Bruck, and Sapin

This is perhaps the best place to insert a short discussion of an "approach" to analysis developed some years ago by Richard Snyder and several of his associates.[13] Though this "approach" owes very little to communications theory and cybernetics, its principal focus is also on decison-making as a process. The authors start from an interest in exploring the genesis of political decisions in the sense of identifying "*some* of the crucial variables that determine . . . responses to concrete situations."[14] In pursuing this objective, Snyder and his associates have laid out a rather formal and extensive framework for the analysis of decision-making. They incorporate concepts from a number of fields including sociology and psychology, and they set forth a typological view of the determinants of decision-making that allows for several levels of analysis. Ultimately this "approach" to the

[12] David Braybooke and Charles E. Lindblom, *A Strategy of Decision* (New York: The Free Press of Glencoe, 1963).
[13] The basic work is conveniently reprinted in Richard C. Snyder, H. W. Bruck, and Burton Sapin (eds.), *Foreign Policy Decision Making* (Glencoe, Ill.: The Free Press, 1963).
[14] *Ibid.*, p. 2.

Approaches from Communications Theory and Cybernetics

nature of decision-making leans more toward the formal tradition of Simon[15] than the *incremental* tradition of Lindblom.[16] The original work on the "approach" was oriented toward the analysis of foreign policy decisions but, as the authors themselves argue, it is formulated in very general terms and is adaptable for the analysis of most types of decision.

Its main thrust is the effort to set up an extensive framework of variables for the analysis of the actual determinants of decision-making. After discussing the need for additional and more systematic conceptualization in this area, the authors proceed to construct a map of variables and clusters of variables for the analysis of decisions. They argue strongly that there is an important need to join together analyses at the level of both the individual and the organization, which accounts for their interest in using material from both psychology and sociology in constructing a unified "approach."

The authors then undertake to provide specific categories for analyzing the determinants of individual acts of decision-making. Their analysis here turns on the delineation of several complex clusters of variables, the first of which focuses on "spheres of competence," including problems of role, role structures, role relations, formal and informal roles, and legitimation. A second cluster fans out under the heading of communication and information, including analysis of information flows, communications networks, information processing, memory, and recall. The third broad cluster centers on motivation, including a variety of subjects dealing with the acquisition of motives, incentives, and expectations.

Underlying this effort to map clusters of relevant variables are several general points of stress. First, the authors emphasize perception and repeatedly seek to distinguish between decision makers' definitions of situations and the more objective facts of reality. Second, the notion of choice is taken as a crucial point in the analysis of any given decision. This concept is used because it avoids any predetermined judgments about the problem of rationality. Third, their "approach" stresses the distinction between structures and processes. As such, it represents an early example of stress on this distinction.

At this point, however, it is important to turn to several problems of this work. Above all, these constructs do not really constitute a full-fledged approach as the term is used in this volume for several reasons. To begin with, the work ultimately amounts to a checklist or taxonomy with little

15 The classic statement appears in Herbert Simon, *Administrative Behavior,* 2nd. ed. (New York: Macmillan, 1961).

16 See Charles E. Lindblom, "The Science of 'Muddling Through,'" *Public Administration Review,* Vol. 29, No. 2 (Spring 1959), pp. 79–88, and Charles E. Lindblom, "Policy Analysis," *American Economic Review,* Vol. XLVIII, No. 3 (June 1958), pp. 298–312.

Approaches from Communications Theory and Cybernetics

effort to specify relations among variables or to rank variables in terms of importance. As a result the authors provide a large number of boxes and classifying schemes with relatively few guidelines for discriminating among them in terms of relevance or importance.[17] Beyond this their constructs are not based on an articulated conception of the nature of politics and of basic political processes. Hence, the logical upshot of this work is a call for specific case studies of individual decisions. But this in turn raises serious problems since a very great number of case studies would be required before reliable generalizations about decision-making could be derived. Finally, the authors have provided such large quantities of variables and such a complex set of boxes that a thorough case study of even one decision is an undertaking of great proportions. In short, they create a "situation in which everything is treated as a variable, in which neither the conditions nor the constants are specified or, alternatively, left to chance."[18] The researcher utilizing these constructs is therefore likely to find little assistance in his efforts to select relevant material from the universe of data and to rank his materials in terms of relative importance.

For all these reasons the decision-making schema of Snyder, Bruck, and Sapin is not especially functional for political analysis in the sense that the term is used in this volume. From the point of view of description, the schema is rich in concepts and constructs. This richness is offset, however, by the inordinate quantity and complexity of concepts and by the failure to provide guidelines for discriminating among them. The conceptions of power and influence are largely traditional. There are some interesting notions concerning goals and objectives as elements of the decison-making process, but little emphasis is placed on the processes of goal setting and goal changing or on the effects of decisions, once taken, on prevailing goals and objectives.

[17] See the review of Snyder, Bruck, and Sapin by Herbert McClosky entitled "Concerning Strategies for a Science of International Politics," which appeared originally in *World Politics*. It is reprinted in Snyder, Bruck, and Sapin (eds.), pp. 186–205. For the specific point consult pp. 199–200.
[18] *Ibid.*, p. 201.

Approaches from Communications Theory and Cybernetics

Distributive Analyses

Another type of decison-making orientation
focuses on the values that are at stake in political
processes and on the allocation or distribution
of these values. This general perspective is encapsulated
in the famous question, "Who gets what, when, how?"
Moreover, the originator of that question,
Harold Lasswell, is responsible for the most extensive
and thoroughly worked-out presentations
of the distributive approach to political

analysis. The present chapter, therefore, focuses on his work as a means of probing the nature of distributive analysis in political science.

The Nature of the Approach

It is important to note that Lasswell takes a broad view of the scope of politics and political processes. He sometimes argues that "The study of politics is the study of influence and the influential."[1] At other times he discusses the scope of political science in terms of power, as in the view that "the subject matter of political science is constituted by power as a process."[2] But he invariably argues that political processes operate *throughout* society and that any attempt to limit political analysis to certain, specific political institutions is unacceptable. This is so because "The power process is not a distinct and separable part of the social process, but only the political aspect of an interactive whole."[3] In this connection, he even suggests that he has consciously attempted "to disseminate a less trammelled conception of political analysis than the one generally current."[4]

The fundamental role accorded to the concepts of influence and power is evident. "The unifying frame of reference for the special student of politics is the rich and variable meaning of 'influence and the influential,' 'power and the powerful.'"[5] Lasswell makes a definite attempt to distinguish these two notions: *influence* is "the value position and potential of a person or group"[6] as measured by a number of indexes; *power,* on the other hand, "is participation in the making of decisions."[7] Here power is viewed in instrumental terms in contrast to its importance as a value in its own right in later stages of Lasswell's analysis. The distinctions drawn here become somewhat less clear, however, as we begin to consider the use or exercise of power and influence as constrasted with their simple existence. "The *exercise of influence* consists in affecting policies of others than the self."[8] And policies can be viewed as meaningful combinations of decisions. At this point it becomes evident that the two concepts are very closely related even though the use of both allows for some interesting conceptual nuances.

[1] Harold Lasswell, *Politics: Who Gets What, When, How* (New York: World Publishing Company, 1958), p. 13.
[2] Harold Lasswell and Abraham Kaplan, *Power and Society* (New Haven: Yale University Press, 1950), p. xvii.
[3] *Ibid.*
[4] Lasswell, *Politics, op. cit.*, p. 203.
[5] *Ibid.*, p. 23.
[6] Lasswell and Kaplan, *op. cit.*, p. 55.
[7] *Ibid.*, p. 75.
[8] *Ibid.*, p. 71.

Distributive Analyses

There are, moreover, a number of key variables that apply equally to influence and power. The *scope* of power or influence refers to the range of values over which control is exercised. *Weight* is the degree of control in the making of decisions or the shaping of policies. And the persons over whom control is exercised constitute the *domain* of power or influence. Similarly, it is important to distinguish between coercive and persuasive exercises of power and influence. Coercion is present in a situation "if the alternative courses of action are associated with severe deprivations or indulgences";[9] in other words, enforced changes in the value position of the relevant actor. Coercion may characterize both influence and power, though Lasswell suggests that severe coercion is especially typical of power processes. Finally, it is worth noting that power and influence include both present and potential capabilities. This is so because all value positions are looked upon as ultimately exchangeable for some amount of power or influence.

Since the focus of the approach turns repeatedly to values and value positions, it is important to clarify these subjects at an early point. In effect, Lasswell treats all human aspirations in terms of a number of central value categories. In his analysis there are eight value categories which are, in turn, divided into two groups of four. Values that emphasize deference or ascribed position include power, respect, rectitude, and affection. Value categories that deal with the welfare of the individual include well-being, wealth, enlightenment, and skill. Upward and downward movement in the various value categories is measured in terms of indulgences and deprivations. At the same time, the concepts of influence and power tie in very closely here since, in their more static form, they ultimately refer to value positions and differentials in these positions.

There are two major views of values that require clarification: values may represent ends in themselves as is the case when individuals seek wealth or power, for example, for themselves; at the same time values may serve as instruments or means for the achievement of other aspirations or goals. The conception of means-ends chains arises from this distinction. This orientation also leads to several other distinctions of importance. First, there are exchange ratios among the various values. Almost any value is usable, at least to some degree, for enhancing one's position in terms of other values. A very common illustration of this point deals with the use of power to attain other ends. Lasswell in fact argues that power is more commonly taken as an instrumental value than as an end in itself. Similarly, other values are exchangeable in this way. Second, there is an interdependence among values. It is difficult to achieve a very high rank in terms of a stated value without having substantial capabilities in terms of

[9] *Ibid.*, p. 98.

other values. Interdependence also emerges from the fact that any given value may be instrumental in the exercise of other values. Thus an actor may have economic power or influence derived from respect. And power can be exercised with skill or enlightenment.

Values and their allocation are the core of the distributive approach in the sense that they deal with the "what" of the question, "who gets what, when, how." Questions concerning "when" and "how" lie at the heart of Lasswell's conception of political processes and are intimately locked in to his complex notions of influence and power. In order to unravel this maze, Lasswell has elaborated a number of orienting conceptual structures.

His most basic conceptual structure for the analysis of political processes centers on the notion of a configurative appro ch leading to contextual analysis. Through this type of analysis he means to give a time-space orientation to the quest of relevant political actors to alter their value positions in desired ways. The aim is to analyze the activities of political actors, interacting in political arenas, and utilizing certain base values and political strategies in order to achieve specified outcomes and long-term effects. An understanding of all the factors that fall under these rubrics will lead, in turn, to an understanding both of the political processes involved in the exercise of power and influence and of the nature of political decision making.

The fundamental unit of analysis in Lasswell's approach is the individual. Groups are aggregates of individuals. Political processes stem essentially from a large number of interpersonal relations that relate to the exercise of power and influence. For this reason contextual analysis must deal largely with individuals, relations among individuals, and the background factors that shape these relations. This orientation allows Lasswell to treat at length a number of variables that are sometimes deemphasized by other political scientists. Individuals are moved by fundamental perspectives and proximate objectives. Their expectations concerning themselves and others are important in shaping their political behavior. Above all, their desired value patterns provide motivating force and lead them to aggregate their interests with those of others wherever there is a substantial degree of overlap.

Individuals operate the political processes of a society within certain arenas "in which power is sought and persons are brought within the domain of power."[10] An arena is therefore a sphere of political interaction. The wherewithal of power and influence within a political arena stems from the possession of base values. Lasswell has defined these in two ways: (1) all of the eight values are usable as base values since, taken as instrumental values, they can be exchanged for power and influence; (2) for

68   [10] *Ibid.*, p. 78.

shorthand purposes Lasswell has sometimes categorized base values in terms of people, institutions, and physical resources available for use in political processes. Actors combine and employ base values on the basis of various strategies. Although specific strategies may be very complex, four basic categories emerge: diplomatic, economic, military, and ideological (or propagandistic).

The immediate results of interactions within the political arena appear in terms of changes in the distribution of values or, in instrumental terms, in the distribution of power and influence—the outcomes of the political process. The political process, however, operates continuously over time and produces a constant stream of outcomes. With the passage of time, certain patterns and trends emerge from these outcomes as longer-term effects of the political process.

Though configurative or contextual analysis is central to the distributive approach, Lasswell has supplemented this orientation with several additional conceptual structures for the analysis of political processes. In terms that are sufficiently general to cover political interactions both in institutional settings and in a variety of less formal arrangements, he has discussed the modalities of transforming influence or power into other values with a focus on characteristic patterns in which power and influence are exercised.

In conceptualizing instruments aimed at controlling the distribution of values, Lasswell has placed a strong emphasis on some of the less tangible factors. To begin with, he stresses the role of *symbols* as tools in the exercise of power and influence. Symbols include ideologies and conceptions of utopia as well as a wide variety of value-laden images and words. The channel for the use of symbols is communication. Through a wide variety of media symbolic habits are instilled, stereotypes are implanted, and propaganda (in the broad sense) is conducted. Similarly, there are many *practices* that become important as instruments in the exercise of power and influence. Practices are "all the ways by which elites are recruited and trained, all the forms observed in policy-making and administration."[11] Long-accepted structural arrangements for government and constitutional provisions are practices. By the same token, various tactics and techniques utilized by elites in political arenas are also practices.

Other modalities of transformation are much more tangible and familiar. The use of physical resources or goods that can be apportioned, withheld, or destroyed offers numerous opportunities for the exercise of power and influence. The classic tactics in the use of goods fall under the headings of pricing and rationing. Finally, violence in all its varieties is especially important in the exercise of political power and influence.

[11] Lasswell, *Politics, op. cit.,* p. 80.

Threats and physical uses of violence, however, raise many important problems of regulation. Unless violence is clearly "subordinated to the total operation of which it is a part,"[12] it can easily become an end in itself, thus losing its instrumental role.

Another set of conceptual structures is much more appropriate for the analysis of formal or institutional settings. At this point the distributive approach focuses more directly on the functions and structures that are generally associated with governmental operations. The approach to these operations is through the concept of decision-making processes. A decision is "The outcome of the shaping of power in an encounter"[13] or interaction within the political arena. And where these processes occur in integrated patterns, it is possible to analyze them in systematic terms.

The process of making decisions breaks down into a sevenfold classification of decision functions. In all of this the unifying theme concerns the development, utilization, and modification of authoritative prescriptions dealing with the distribution and enjoyment of values. The process begins with the gathering of intelligence about present conditions, goals, and policies for their attainment. Interested parties then make recommendations concerning the need for prescriptions and afterwards lobby for their acceptance in the appropriate governmental structures. Following this some of the recommendations are accepted and transformed into formal prescriptions. Once prescriptions come into existence there remains the problem of utilizing them. Invocation deals with the provisional application of prescriptions to concrete situations, and final application refers to the authoritative matching of prescriptions with concrete situations. Politics, however, is a continuous process, and prescriptions must constantly be adapted to meet changing circumstances. Appraisal is therefore necessary to assess the extent to which prescriptions are, in fact, relevant to actual conditions and operating to achieve goals. And finally, some prescriptions must be terminated or modified to make way for new prescriptions that will operate more effectively in the effort to attain goals.

It is in this context that Lasswell introduces a number of problems that have traditionally been of concern to political scientists. He deals with questions of authority and legitimacy in terms of the decision-making process that characterizes the operations of government. Similarly, the differences between authoritative and effective control appears in this connection. An authoritative decision-making system is one whose actions are perceived as legitimate, whereas effectiveness concerns operational efficacy rather than legitimacy. There are, of course, connections between the two, and a stable government is likely to possess both. Moreover, this

[12] *Ibid.*, p. 60.
[13] Lasswell and Kaplan, *op. cit.*, p. 81.

Distributive Analyses

format allows for the introduction of a wide range of questions dealing, for example, with forms of government, structural arrangements, and operating procedures under the general heading of ruling practices.

Lasswell has structured his approach with an eye toward certain substantive and methodological problems that have held his attention over the years. Some of these particular interests deserve mention here since they have shaped certain aspects of the general approach and since they are illustrative of the concerns that grow out of the perspectives associated with Lasswell.

In substantive terms Lasswell has always been interested in psychology and the interactions between political processes and personality types. His basic unit, as previously stated, is the individual, and his emphasis has always been on "interpersonal relations, not abstract institutions or organizations."[14] Even his long-standing interest in such social phenomena as class developments and the nature of groups must be seen from the basic perspective of individuals. Though social aggregates occupy an important place in some of his work, such aggregates are ultimately composed of individuals pursuing interpersonal relations in various contexts. Beyond this, Lasswell's conceptualizations are richly oriented toward a variety of somewhat intangible *cultural* variables. Much attention is devoted to many aspects of symbols, political myths, ideologies, and utopias. Likewise, intangible political practices, mores, and patterns of perspectives and attitudes occupy an important place. These concerns are, of course, traceable to a focus on the individual as the basic unit, but they are mediated through a variety of human interactions and political processes.

Lasswell's approach also shows the impact of certain long-standing methodological concerns. His interests in systematic data gathering and in what he has called mapping exercises are an important factor behind the formalism and systematic structuring of his principal conceptions. In this connection it is important not only to spell out variables in clear terms but also to state the relationships among variables as systematically as possible. These concerns are reinforced by the so-called index problem. *Index instability* occurs in situations where the connections between abstract concepts and experiential situations are ambiguous, variable, and subject to diverse interpretations. Though this frustrating problem cannot be entirely avoided in the social sciences, the first rule in reducing it calls for the maximum clarification of definitions, concepts, and propositions before they are applied to empirical material. A further methodological interest concerns the usefulness of trend analyses. Lasswell has for a long time been interested in the strong sense of dynamism or flow that characterizes even very stable polities. In a context of underlying continuity coupled with

[14] *Ibid.,* p. xxiv.

Distributive Analyses

substantial change, trend analyses are likely to reach their maximum utility. And upon inspection, it seems reasonable to suggest that the main thrust of the distributive approach is toward conditions of this kind.

Finally, Lasswell's approach is deeply influenced by his interest in policy-oriented inquiry. The relevant distinction here is between a manipulative standpoint and a contemplative one. Manipulative inquiry concerns itself with the selection of goals in a given context; the analysis of alternative courses of action and background conditions relating to the achievement of goals; and the decision processes by which concrete courses of action are chosen from the existing alternatives. Such a posture tends to lead to an interest in active participation in political processes. The contemplative approach, on the other hand, focuses on relations of interdependence among variables and on explanation in terms of causal connections. Here understanding achieves significance in terms of the ongoing inquiry itself. Lasswell quite rightly argues that it is not necessary to make a definite choice between these postures; "both manipulative and contemplative standpoints may be adopted."[15] His own approach, however, is very much oriented toward the analysis of policies and policy making. In short, he conceives of "political science as one of the policy sciences—that which studies influence and power."[16]

Functions of the Approach

Lasswell's distributive approach to politics is complex and rather meticulously worked out. At the level of abstract formulations, therefore, it does not suffer from some of the tentative and rough qualities that mark certain other approaches, a fact which facilitates the evaluative tasks addressed in this section.

In terms of the various analytic types of approach outlined in Chapter One, Lasswell's work falls rather well down the scale in the direction of deductive formulation. He is acutely conscious of the need for clear-cut and systematic definitions from which it is possible to develop first conceptual structures and then propositions. This tendency, which is evident throughout Lasswell's work, comes out most clearly in *Power and Society,* where the format demands a largely deductive process of reasoning. It is of course true that both the concepts and the propositions of the approach owe a lot to the previously available literature of political science with which Lasswell has long been thoroughly familiar. He himself speaks, for example, of "reformulations, as hypotheses to be subjected to inquiry, of

[15] *Ibid.,* p. xi.
[16] *Ibid.,* p. xii.

the content of political prudence."[17] The principal point, however, is that "this working knowledge must be recast in theoretical terms to serve the ends of political inquiry,"[18] and here Lasswell has chosen to follow a largely deductive course.

Interestingly, there is no assumption that the resultant propositions will necessarily conform closely with subsequent empirical analysis; this is not their main function.

> Since the propositions are taken as regulative hypotheses, not formulations of established laws, we are not concerned with marshaling evidence supposed to establish them. They are intended to serve the functions of directing the search for significant data, not of predicting what the data will be found to disclose.[19]

At the same time, this suggests Lasswell's long-standing and deep concern with empirical analysis. Empirical work is not undertaken only to verify set propositions—an analytic approach must serve to guide and fructify forays into the realm of experiential data and not merely to provide testable propositions. Work on the approach, nevertheless, must precede empirical analysis and be substantially deductive, since its control and regulative functions in the realm of empirical data would otherwise deteriorate.

This brings us to the breakdown of categories elaborated in Chapter One. As concerns descriptive usefulness, Lasswell's distributive approach is controversial. Critics often complain that the approach is so self-consciously conceptual as to be top heavy with categories and variables at the expense of analytic insights. Others suggest that an excessive concern with definitional nuances has led to a loss of contact with real world problems. On the other hand, there is much to recommend Lasswell's approach in descriptive terms. It is very rich in sheer quantity of concepts, and its self-consciousness often leads to a clarification of otherwise ambiguous problems. Most significantly, however, one finds time and again that a skillful manipulator of the distributive concepts is able to develop insights and fruitful questions simply by applying the framework to substantive problems. While it may be important to think in terms of a selective utilization of the descriptive material from this approach, it can provide considerable descriptive power if handled well.

Problems of pattern maintenance and regulation are largely deemphasized in the distributive approach. Questions along these lines stem especially from systemic conceptions and from perspectives that emphasize

---

[17] *Ibid.*, p. xxii. "Political prudence" is Charles Merriam's phrase to designate common sense beliefs and commonly accepted views about politics.
[18] *Ibid.*
[19] *Ibid.*, p. xxiii.

Distributive Analyses

the interaction of social forces, both of which are largely absent from the work of Lasswell. He does speak from time to time of problems of stability, especially relating to the operations of various types of regime or rule as contrasted with over-all political systems. And he specifically contrasts *equilibrium* and *developmental analysis,* though the latter continually comes in for more attention than the former. On balance then the approach is not particularly rich in this area.

Turning to patterns of control, one strikes right into the core of the distributive approach. As indicated in the preceding section, this approach conceptualizes the basic political processes in terms of the utilization of power and influence to affect the distribution of values in a society. This is the key to what Lasswell terms the configurative approach to the understanding of politics and to his conception of contextual analysis. The approach devotes more space to the conceptualization of problems in this area than in any other area. The basic building block in the analysis of power and influence is the individual, a posture that leads in turn to a great deal of emphasis on interpersonal relations. Starting from this base, Lasswell moves skillfully on to the analysis of power and influence in large-scale political operations. Groups are basically aggregates of individuals, and institutions are "integrated patterns of practice"[20] carried out by large numbers of individuals. Though allowance is made for various aspects of group behavior, Lasswell's conceptions of power and influence remain as very sophisticated formulations of an approach that begins with the individual.

The broad area of goal attainment forms the second principal pillar of the distributive approach. Lasswell has devoted a great deal of attention to problems concerning the nature of values, their role in human behavior patterns, their attainment in social contexts, and their utilization in a hierarchical fashion. Curiously, he has written very little about the sources of human values and the channels by which they rise to the level of human consciousness. His elaborate classification of values into eight categories is intended more as a stylized but analytically adequate description of the relevant universe of values in human discourse. Along with many useful concepts in this area, Lasswell's lengthy discussion raises interesting problems concerning the relations between individual value orderings and socially defined scales of values. Focusing on the individual as his basic unit makes him receptive to the analysis of goal-attainment from the perspective of the individual. For some time, however, Lasswell has shown an interest in the "values of society as a whole"[21] and in the social determination of value preferences through political processes. This naturally raises many

[20] *Ibid.,* p. 177.
[21] *Ibid.,* p. xii.

Distributive Analyses

questions concerning possible redistribution of the values of a society and effective participation in decisions dealing with such matters. The approach's concepts of power and influence are useful in discussing these problems, but one would hope that Lasswell himself will devote more attention to them in the future.

The approach assumes a somewhat diffuse and differentiated stance in regard to questions of change and political dynamics. Throughout Lasswell's work there is an underlying sense of interest in political flows and dynamics—he has a deep interest in trends and patterns of change. To some extent the distributive focus on value-transformations and decision-making as *keys* to the political process imparts a sense of movement to this orientation. Morever, Lasswell himself has added a sense of interest in political cycles, crises, and rise-and-fall phenomena. He has written at some length, for example, on revolutionary changes in political regimes. Similarly, he has taken an interest in changing class patterns and practices and in the resultant effects on political elites. The distributive approach, however, never focuses very clearly on the problems of fundamental contextual changes. Regimes and practices may change, even violently, but the fundamental political order is generally treated as a given or constant. All the dynamic processes of distribution take place within such a context. For this reason the approach is not rich in conceptual material concerning the problems of political decline and breakdown of existing structures.

Before this section ends, a few words are in order on Lasswell's conception of intellectual tasks. In the course of elaborating his approach and pursuing his own interests, Lasswell has developed a fivefold classification of tasks for political analysis. The analysis of *goals* clarifies the objects of political processes and separates normative questions from empirical operations. *Trend* analyses deal with changes in the distribution of values and in the operations of political processes over time. An emphasis on *conditions* refers to an interest in the scientific effort to explain relationships and trends and in the problems of empirical verification. *Projections* represent an effort to delineate the probable course of developments in the future. Finally, the analysis of *policy alternatives* deals with the selection of courses of action designed to maximize the realization of specified values in the future.

This formulation of intellectual tasks has several interesting characteristics. To begin with, its close association with a manipulative or policy-oriented perspective on political analysis demonstrates Lasswell's fundamental preferences in this area. Within such a framework, however, the formulation is useful since it has allowed Lasswell to organize his various interests into a coherent whole. At the same time, the resultant orientation says little about concrete methodology and is therefore not restrictive in these terms. The analyst still remains free to experiment with a wide range of methods as Lasswell himself has done.

A Critique of Distributive Analyses

As usual, there are problems and pitfalls to be noted. There is, however, an interesting question of value orientation in this case that does not appear so clearly in the discussion of other approaches. Lasswell's work is marked by a noticeable commitment to a kind of liberal, democratic political ethos. He is interested in "the formulation of conditions favorable to the establishment and continuance of a free society,"[22] which implies an effort to formulate and implement various liberal policies as well as a general interest in "human dignity and the realization of human capacities."[23] Lasswell also argues in favor of maximum popular participation in the shaping and sharing of values; in other words, in basic political processes. Evidence of this general value orientation appears in Lasswell's distributive approach at many points. Nevertheless, it does not seriously prejudice the utilization of the approach in most areas. The bulk of the concepts and propositions of the approach are sufficiently separable to be applied even if one assumes a more contemplative posture toward political analysis. At the same time some sense of values is often helpful for illustrative purposes and for the maintenance of meaningful connections with real world problems. The presence of values is, of course, particularly important in the area of policy-oriented research.

Perhaps the most serious intrinsic problems with the distributive approach stem from its extensiveness and almost overwhelming complexity. This leads in particular to problems of formalism and of the proliferation of concepts and conceptual boxes. Formalism in this case originates in Lasswell's concern for definitional clarity and for a large number of rather fine distinctions and nuances. Such an orientation is helpful up to a point, but it leads to problems when carried to extremes. The world of empirical reality is in fact often ambiguous and is generally not characterized by clear boundaries and sharp distinctions. Conceptual distinctions sometimes lead to insights difficult to derive from the fuzzy quality of empirical readings. Difficulties arise, however, because formalism, when carried too far, leads to ever greater gaps between abstract formulations and real world phenomena.

Another problem that arises is that of proliferation. The distributive approach encompasses a number of very complex conceptual structures,

[22] *Ibid.*, p. xiii.
[23] *Ibid.*, p. xxiv.

Distributive Analyses

and to make matters worse, Lasswell has tended to develop additional complexes of concepts that are only fully meaningful when juxtaposed to the original structures in a fashion that produces multiples of the previous number of conceptual boxes. The net effect of this procedure is almost overwhelming for the analyst contemplating a new area of research. Moreover, after a certain point it becomes increasingly dysfunctional. One of the functions of an approach to analysis is to select material for study from the vast quantity of potential data and to provide criteria with which to differentiate between important and unimportant material. It is obviously useful to have a rich conceptual matrix to apply to these tasks, but an approach that results in an excessive number of conceptual structures and boxes eventually leads the analyst into a vicious circle in terms of his problems of selection.

Related to these difficulties is the general problem of discursiveness. Because the distributive approach has an enormous range of conceptual material and because it is difficult to use certain parts of it in isolation, those who utilize the approach are faced with a dilemma: If they use the approach to its full extent in analyzing a given set of problems, they will end up with massive volumes of material that may also tend to be somewhat disjointed. If, on the other hand, they employ the approach less thoroughly, their results are likely to have a desultory quality. Though they may often be suggestive, they will exhibit a tendency to treat any given subject only by way of a few illustrations before dropping it to move on to other problems. For this reason the analyst, who must also concern himself with very real problems arising from resource limitations, will often find himself in a bind. Though this problem is by no means absolute, it has repeatedly harrassed users of the approach.

There are also several more substantive problems that deserve mention. First, those who utilize the distributive approach sometimes fall into problems of reification in regard to social variables and entities. Lasswell himself escapes many of these difficulties by a very careful process of constructing his analysis of social phenomena on a foundation of psychological concepts and interpersonal connectives. Even then, however, problems sometimes arise as, for example, in the analysis of societal values. Reification is a real problem for users of the approach who, though interested in the allocation and distribution of values, are less well trained in social-psychological *concepts* and generally more interested in social *forces*.

Beyond this, the distributive approach tends to focus attention on various elites and strata of the population that are truly influential. This is partly because Lasswell himself has worked quite extensively in these areas and led the way in applying the distributive approach to them. But there are several specific attributes of the approach itself that thrust in this direction. The combination of a key stress on power and influence on the one hand and a perspective that insists on the individual as the basic unit of analysis on the other leads to an emphasis on elites. One could perhaps profitably study individuals with very little influence from this standpoint, but the resultant work would be bound to remain sketchy and tentative. The study of an equal number of members of an elite would yield results that are far more concrete and general. Moreover, many of the distributive concepts, though relatively operational for the study of elites, become increasingly nebulous when applied to the more amorphous world of political processes among the masses. Again, this is a problem that can be compensated for and substantially alleviated by an adroit manipulation of the distributive approach. It does, nevertheless, constitute an important built-in thrust of the approach that results in a significant pitfall.

Distributive Analyses

Group Theory

Group theory is the common name for one of the more
widely utilized, and controversial, of the current approaches
to political analysis. The intellectual antecedents
of the approach lie in the work of a number
of nineteenth- and early twentieth-century English
philosophers who developed the doctrines
of pluralism. Writers such as Figgis, Maitland, and Cole,
largely as a reaction to the prevailing
tenets of atomistic liberalism and idealist socialism,

elaborated the notion that the group is the basic unit of society.[1] The result was a philosophical and deductive theory of pluralism.

It remained, however, for twentieth-century social science to undertake a systematic conceptualization of the role of groups in social systems that might be labeled *analytic pluralism*. As a result the approach has achieved a considerable impact in a number of social science disciplines. In political science the systematic development of group theory dates from the publication of Arthur Bentley's *The Process of Government* in 1908. The publication of this volume was followed, nevertheless, by a long period of quiescence during which political scientists took little interest in the possibilities of utilizing group theory on a systematic basis. But this situation began to change in the 1940's when a number of important analysts began to pick up the basic conceptions of Bentley and to explore the possibilities of a group theory of politics. The connection between Bentley and this later generation of group theorists should not of course be overemphasized. The latter have branched out in a number of directions and sometimes proceeded far afield from the original conception of a group theory of politics. At the same time, the similarities among these writers are sufficiently strong to set them off from other analysts of political phenomena and to justify speaking, at least loosely, of a single approach called group theory. Curiously enough, Bentley's own work remains very important as a systematic statement of the conceptual underpinnings of group theory. Accordingly, his formulations will be referred to rather frequently in the present discussion.

Like many other approaches, the version of group theory that appeared in political science originated as a reaction to certain prevailing practices in the field. To understand the fundamental conceptions of the theory, it should be helpful to clarify these reactive features of the approach at the outset. The emphasis on dynamics and processes in group theory is essentially a criticism of the formalism and static quality of the institutional approach to political analysis that was prevalent in the early twentieth century. In addition, the tenacious insistence of group theorists on the central position of the group was a reaction not only to the atomistic individualism of the so-called classical liberals but also to a kind of simple psychologism that purported to deal with social events in terms of human ideas and ideals without a very adequate theory of perception. These reactive elements of group theory have been of considerable importance in shaping applications of the approach throughout its history in political science.

[1] The main thrust of atomistic liberalism, in this context, stems from the work of Locke and Bentham. The idealist socialists were led by Green and Bosanquet. In this perspective, Mill would fall somewhere in the middle ground.

Group Theory

The Principal Concepts of Group Theory

The fundamental unit of analysis in the theory is the human group. It is important at the outset to pin down quite carefully the exact sense in which group theorists use this concept. In the words of Bentley, a group

. . . means a certain portion of the men of a society, taken, however, not as a physical mass cut off from other masses of men, but as a mass [of] activity, which does not preclude the men who participate in it from participating likewise in many other group activities.[2]

There are several points worth stressing about this conception of a group. Most importantly, a group is seen as a mass of activity and not as a collection of individuals; as a patterned process rather than a static form. A group does not emerge unless the interactions among the individual members are both relatively frequent and sufficiently patterned to produce directional activity.[3] A genuine group is therefore to be distinguished both from a coincidental collection and from a "categoric group."[4] At the same time it is important to note that individuals will hold simultaneous memberships in a number of groups with varying degrees of intensity. This fact is not only significant in analyzing the interactions among groups, it is also a key factor in necessitating the conceptualization of individual groups as patterns of activity rather than as collections of individuals.

Another critical aspect of the group lies in the notion of *interest*—a shared attitude concerning a claim or claims to be made by one group upon certain other groups in a social system. At the same time the problem of locating and defining group interests is treated positivistically.[5] The interest of a group is taken to be the sum of its policy-oriented and directional activities.[6] There is therefore no need for external standards in measuring group interests. For this reason, also, all groups must necessarily have one or more interests and, by definition, no group can act in a way that is incompatible with its own interests.[7] As a result the notion of interest

[2] Arthur F. Bentley, *The Process of Government* (Chicago: University of Chicago Press, 1908), p. 211.
[3] On this point consult David Truman, *The Governmental Process* (New York: Knopf, 1964), p. 23.
[4] A categoric group refers to a number of individuals who share one or more characteristics but who do not interact with any degree of frequency. Thus high school students, blondes, and truck drivers all constitute categoric groups.
[5] On this point see Charles B. Hagan, "The Group in a Political Science," in Roland Young (ed.), *Approaches to the Study of Politics* (Evanston, Ill.: Northwestern University Press, 1958), p. 46.
[6] *Ibid.*, p. 45.
[7] Bentley, *op. cit.*, p. 211.

Group Theory

actually comes within the scope of the fundamental definition of group in this system. As the group theorists themselves sometimes put it, an interest is really one aspect, the directional one, of the mass of activity that *is* a group. On the other hand, the group theorists do occasionally suggest that at any given time there may be various interests that are not actually attached to any group and are therefore unrepresented. The apparent incongruity of this notion accounts for such concepts as potential groups, latent groups, and groups in a stage of "becoming" that are employed in some form by most of the group theorists.

The real core of the group approach, however, is found in the analysis of the interaction processes of the very large number of groups that make up a social system. As Bentley puts it, "The society itself is nothing other than the complex of groups that compose it."[8] The total meaning and fabric of a social system can be understood as a "sort of mosaic of groups"[9] constantly interacting with each other. The engine that makes a social system run is the process of group struggle through which all the various groups seek to realize or maximize their interests. The result is a kind of boiling cauldron of activity, characterized by a shifting balance of influence among a wide variety of groups. As Latham argues, society is "a single universe of groups which combine, break, federate, and form coalitions and constellations of power in a flux of restless alterations."[10]

Several aspects of this conception of society require emphasis. First, though the engine of society is "the push and resistance between groups," the state of society at any given time is constituted by the "balance of the group pressures."[11] Second, while the individual group is the fundamental unit of analysis in this approach, groups only gain their full meaning in relation to other groups. A labor organization, for example, can only be fully understood in terms of its relations with one or more firms or employers' associations. Third, this conception of society is generally completed in detail with both horizontal and vertical conceptualizations of groups and group relations. It is necessary to deal not only with a wide range of different types of groups coexisting on the same plane but also with the phenomenon of layered patterns of groups, some of which "reflect" or "represent" the interests of others. Fourth, this whole conception of society is based upon the critical significance of processes rather than of specific structures or substantive content (values). The *dynamics* of the interaction process constitute the fundamental facts.

[8] *Ibid.*, p. 222.
[9] Truman, *op. cit.*, p. 32.
[10] Earl Latham, *The Group Basis of Politics* (Ithaca, New York: Cornell University Press, 1952), p. 49.
[11] Bentley, *op. cit.*, pp. 258–259.

Group Theory

Within this framework there is room for a rich variety of descriptive categories and concepts dealing with the organization and activity of various groups. For purposes of brief characterization, these concepts may be divided into three broad sets. To begin with, there is a great deal of interest in the internal organization and processes of various groups. Questions concerning boundary conditions, size, territoriality, and forms of integration are relevant here. So is the range of questions dealing with degrees of organization, hierarchies, patterns of control, and fluidity of membership. Here also belongs Truman's distinction between ordinary groups and associations, which are "groups formed around tangent relations."[12]

A second broad set of concepts concerns the position of a group in the over-all system of groups composing a society. Important in this sense are concepts dealing with the vertical separation of groups into various layers, problems concerning overlapping or cross-cutting memberships, and questions dealing with patterns of alliances and coalitions among groups. The underlying problem is the attempt to define the meaning of individual groups in terms of their external relations in a system of groups.

Another set of concepts that has occupied much of the attention of a number of group theorists focuses on the techniques and tactics of influence. On the one hand, there are numerous concepts dealing with group strength, power, and the factors of power such as (1) the number of members in a group, (2) the intensity of concern with a given interest, and (3) the forms of organization utilized by various groups. On the other hand, interest sometimes focuses more precisely on the tactics used by different groups in a variety of contexts.[13] Analyses of such matters as forms of leadership, the uses of propaganda, the manipulation of public opinion, and pressure tactics belong under this heading.

Given such a group approach to society, what is the realm of politics and political behavior? There is a certain amount of ambiguity in group theory about this subject. Many of the group theorists have followed Bentley's lead in arguing against making early definitions of politics and for a program of simply going forward with the analysis of interesting subjects that seem to fall roughly within the realm commonly understood as politics.[14] This, however, has led to certain ambiguities in the conceptions of

---

[12] Truman, op. cit., p. 41. An association develops when members or representatives of two or more groups join to defend certain interests that are disturbed or threatened by a third group. For example, a PTA joins parents and teachers together to deal with problems attendant upon teaching children, and a labor association brings workers from several plants together to deal with the problems of defending common interests against employers.

[13] By far the largest portion of Truman's book focuses on such questions.

[14] On this position consult Bentley, op. cit., p. 199.

Group Theory

group theory. Bentley apparently viewed politics as a rather high-level activity carried on largely by groups that somehow reflect or represent the underlying forces in a society.[15] Other analysts, however, visualize political activity as simply one part or aspect of the total actiivty of individual groups. Groups are here arrayed more nearly on a horizontal plane. Nor is it always clear whether the group theorists see groups as operating within some kind of otherwise established political context, or themselves constituting the political context as the sum of their politically relevant activities.

An approach to this problem that some of the group theorists employ involves the importation of an external definition of politics to distinguish between the political and nonpolitical segments of the : over-all mass of group activities. Truman, for example, suggests that politics is involved when groups make their claims "through or upon the institutions of government."[16] Latham, on the other hand, argues more broadly that politics is involved in all the processes in a society leading to the allocation of values through structures of power.[17] Though this definitional procedure is not entirely satisfactory, it may be a necessary device since the group conception of society involves a kind of seamless web of constant group interactions.

At the same time there is a *de facto* sense in which almost all of the group theorists have opted for a rather broad view of the nature of politics. As a function of their conception of society, they are all concerned very basically with power and the processes of group struggle and adjustment. And these phenomena occur all over the map of society. Latham, for example, recognizes this problem explicitly when he talks about politics in a public sense in connection with the formal institutions of government— as distinct from politics in a private sense involving the adjustment of claims through power structures external to government. In the final analysis, then, political behavior tends to have something to do with the adjustment of conflicting group claims through the use of power in a wide variety of contexts.

Beyond this somewhat generalized conception of politics, group theory includes some interesting conceptions of the more specific nature and functions of government. There is also, however, a certain ambiguity concerning the exact dimensions of government. Bentley himself distinguished three senses of the word government, ranging from a conception that would make government more or less coincident with all the processes of adjustment among groups in a given society to a much narrower view in which government seems to coincide much more nearly with the institu-

[15] *Ibid.*, p. 209.
[16] Truman, *op. cit.*, p. 505.
[17] See Latham, *op. cit.*, pp. 12–16.

Group Theory

tions (seen of course as masses of activity) traditionally included in the more formal definitions of government.[18] The result is somewhat obscure since the broadest of these views makes government more or less coequal with politics in general, while the narrowest view is too limited to be fully congruent with the other elements of group theory.

A common theme about government that does, nevertheless, emerge from the work of almost all the group theorists is that government has something to do with the establishment of regularized adjustment processes for handling the struggle among political interest groups. Two aspects of this governmental function deserve specific mention. First, government often functions as a mediator in the struggle among groups and as a source of rules and restraints. As Truman states this role, "government functions to establish and maintain a measure of order in the relationships among groups."[19] Second, government frequently provides a forum within which the group struggle can proceed in the presence of certain overarching boundaries and limits. This forum role is, of course, typical of legislatures but it also occurs to a considerable extent within the other branches of government. Among other things, this view of government provides an interesting comparative perspective. Group theory has little use for the traditional classification schemes that have been used to distinguish types of government. Instead it suggests that governments should be both distinguished and compared in terms of differences in the mechanisms and processes of adjustment that they provide for the purpose of handling the ongoing struggle of political interest groups.[20]

At the same time the basic logic of group theory demands a somewhat more complicated view of the nature of government. Just as society is composed of interacting groups, government itself is actually composed of a number of groups. In addition to functioning as an adjustor of the over-all group struggle in society, government tends to harbor a variety of groups that are themselves often in conflict with each other. For this reason government is (1) a microcosm of broader social processes, (2) often a source of interests and claims that become ingredients in the total political processes of a society, and (3) a multifaceted mass of activity offering a variety of points of access to outside groups.[21] A problem arises at this point, however, in regard to the development of criteria distinguishing the realm of government from the more general group struggle in society. This problem has essentially been confronted in two ways: (1) in terms of

---

[18] Bentley, *op. cit.*, pp. 260–262.
[19] Truman, *op. cit.*, p. 45.
[20] On this subject consult Bentley, *op. cit.*, Chapter XII.
[21] The subject of access comes up repeatedly in Truman's analysis. For a general discussion see Truman, *op. cit.*, pp. 264–270.

Group Theory

concepts such as Latham's notion of "officiality," which distinguishes government in terms of its authoritative stature in the eyes of the other actors in the social system;[22] (2) in terms of an appeal to the prevailing common sense or lexical notions of the province of government.

Given this conception of society and politics as a constant struggle among groups, what is it that keeps the whole system on an even keel and that prevents it from breaking down under the weight of ever more extensive group conflicts?[23] Group theory offers several lines of explanation in this area. The competing groups that make up society are seen as participating in an unconscious balancing process. The vast mosaic of competing groups and the existence of divergent lines of conflict guarantee that all individual groups will be kept in check by the simultaneous activities of other groups. Two additional factors support this balance. The government of course plays its role as an adjustor of many group conflicts. In addition, however, the notion of potential groups is brought in as a balancing factor. Any society contains many potential groups that are likely to be activated if one (or more) of the existing groups begins to become too powerful in relation to its competitors. In the very process of gaining strength a group is likely to trespass on a number of latent interests and therefore to activate potential groups. This process constitutes a kind of built-in stabilizing mechanism that operates to keep the group struggle within certain bounds.

A further stabilizing force stems from the phenomenon of overlapping or cross-cutting memberships.[24] Since individuals commonly belong to a number of groups, they are generally unwilling to lend any single group their undivided support. Moreover, they are likely to restrict their support for a group that makes claims which compromise their positions in other groups. The normal result is a highly variegated pattern of cross-cutting cleavages that tends to reduce the intensity of any single axis of conflict. Unless the divisions within a society are such that most important groups will align themselves on one or the other side of a few underlying issues, the very multiplicity of conflicts and overlapping memberships will tend to reduce the intensity of any given conflict and therefore to facilitate the achievement of a state of dynamic equilibrium.

The balance within a society is also powerfully supported by what group theorists call the *rules of the game* (or in Bentley's phrase the "habit background").[25] The rules of the game are seen as unorganized though widely accepted interests that set up certain criteria of acceptability for the

[22] Latham, *op. cit.*, pp. 33–40.
[23] For a general discussion of this subject from the group perspective see Truman, *op. cit.*, pp. 516 ff.
[24] *Ibid.*, pp. 520–522.
[25] *Ibid.*, pp. 512–524.

Group Theory

conduct of intergroup conflict and that are capable of active organization in the event that these criteria are seriously violated. In formal terms, therefore, these rules are potential groups of a very powerful sort. Though the rules are often quiescent in the processes of group interaction that constitute a society, they operate to define and support the adjustment operations normally carried out by government, and they constitute a kind of anticipatory sanction on the activities of most groups since they are capable of activation with very influential results.

Functions of Group Theory

At this point the group theorists' use of the term *theory* requires clarification. Though group theory has become the common name for work utilizing this approach, the essential elements of the approach itself do not fulfill the more formal requirements of theory in either a deductive or an inductive sense. Nor have such claims been made for the approach by many of its leading exponents. Bentley himself was quite clear on this point and explicitly denied any claim to have produced a theory. He insisted, in fact, that his own work constituted an "attempt to fashion a tool"[26] and that his references to real world examples were illustrative rather than definitive. What Bentley did claim was that the group approach would provide a systematic orientation toward political phenomena and that it would be a useful aid in generating questions and hypotheses for detailed investigation. In a general way most of the later group analysts have accepted this basic characterization of the approach, although some of them have been tempted to make additional claims for group theory, at least implicitly. Even Truman, for example, occasionally demonstrates a tendency to incorporate the language of empirical generalization into his more abstract and conceptual passages.

It is interesting to note that, from the beginning, the group theorists have displayed a strong interest in empiricism and in the creation of an approach to analysis that would lend itself to empirical investigations. Bentley himself was extremely impatient with the form of philosophical deductivism prevalent in his day. In contrast, he frequently called for systematic analysis, scientific procedures, and attention to the problems of measurement. Yet Bentley's own empiricism was of a somewhat naive variety since he never fully confronted a number of the problems of operationalizing his concepts. As a result these problems were left largely to the more recent generation of group theorists; and they continue to plague many efforts to employ group theory in concrete empirical investigations.

[26] Bentley considered this point so important that he let it stand alone as the preface to *The Process of Government*.

Group Theory

Similarly, the group approach is couched in language suggesting a strong interest in comparative analysis. It purports to offer concepts that go to the essence of all social and political processes and that are therefore applicable to any society. Here too, however, there are problems. The fact that the approach was developed largely by persons interested in the American political system has left a considerable imprint on its conceptualizations. Several problems of this type will be emphasized at a later point in this chapter.

For further analysis of the functions of group theory, it is necessary to turn once again to the general categories of political analysis utilized in previous chapters. The fact that political scientists have utilized the concepts of group theory somewhat more frequently than concepts of certain other approaches makes this task easier. One of the principal attractions of group theory lies in its descriptive powers. This aspect of the approach has several facets. First, the basic group concepts of society and politics are couched in terms providing a large number of channels for additional conceptualization and categorization of a more detailed sort. Second, the group approach offers novel perspectives by breaking with the more traditional and formalistic categories, but it does so without resorting to highly esoteric or obscure concepts. Third, the group perspective is appealing in the sense that it is possible to lend substance to many of its categories with interesting examples. Though all this does not establish the comprehensiveness of group theory's descriptive powers, it does explain some of the appeal of the approach for many practicing analysts.

Group theory's concern with the problems of pattern maintenance is somewhat ambiguous. The approach envisions the problems of instability and potential breakdown, and it suggests a number of mechanisms that are relevant to the maintenance of a society composed of conflicting groups. At the same time, many of these concepts are never worked out in detail, and the approach's conception of society appears ultimately to imply a kind of "unseen hand" of the type that was demanded by the classical theories of economics. Group theory does, of course, touch on the adjustment functions of government, the conflict dampening role of overlapping group memberships, and the limiting role of rules of the game. But what is to prevent groups from aligning themselves around a few axes of conflict in such a way that the cross-cutting phenomenon does not materialize? And how is it possible for those potential groups, which compose the rules of the game, to operate effectively in a loosely integrated or deeply divided society?

A somewhat similar situation arises with regard to questions concerning patterns of control. Some forms of the group approach suggest an extended interest in the problems of power and influence in the context of

Group Theory

individual groups. A large number of concepts attempt to delve into questions concerning group strength, leadership, techniques of influence, the use of propaganda, and so forth. At the same time, however, interest in control problems fades when one moves beyond the level of the individual group as the fundamental unit of action. The functions of government, for example, are conceptualized more in terms of adjustment and mediation than in terms of control and power. This orientation is, of course, necessitated by group theory's explanation of all social and political phenomena in terms of the interaction of individual groups. But it does not always seem to cover the full range of relevant questions about patterns of control.

The notions of goals and goal attainment are fundamental to the group approach to society. Groups are impelled by their interests and claims upon other groups in the system to participate in the group struggle that constitutes society. In this perspective the drive for goal attainment is the motivating force of the whole process. At the same time, however, group theory adopts a procedural rather than a substantive interest in goals for the most part. The processes of goal seeking are basic, but relatively little attention is paid to the ways in which goals are formulated, articulated, and adopted by various groups. The group approach deals with much of this latter area in a definitional fashion—a group's interests (and therefore its goals) are taken to be the sum of its directional activities. The positivism of this orientation tends to reduce interest in the sources and development of political goals.

Problems of change also constitute a very important concern of the group approach. Since all social phenomena are conceptualized in terms of masses of activity and dynamic processes, change is a fundamental and pervasive fact of social existence. The processes of group interaction that constitute society imply a constantly shifting balance of group relationships together with an ever present interplay of actions consciously aimed at bringing about changes in the distribution of values in a society. *Change* is therefore one of the fundamental facts of the group approach. Nevertheless, it is important to note that this concern with change relates primarily to "middle range" changes rather than to more fundamental or systemic changes. Change envisioned by group theory goes on primarily within the bounds of a basically stable system and relates to the shifting balances among individual groups in the system. The approach ultimately has relatively little to say about the more basic changes involved in system transformation.

A Critique of Group Theory

In recent years group theory has become a source of considerable controversy and critical debate, and the fact that the approach has influenced the organization of a number of important research enterprises has only served to stimulate this debate. The charges leveled against group theory fall into several distinguishable categories. First, a number of criticisms focus directly on intrinsic features of the approach. Second, there are charges (such as the complaint against Bentley's naive empiricism) that are more relevant to the failings of individual practitioners than to the intrinsic nature of the approach itself. Third, there are charges emanating from an overextended conception of the nature of the approach. The charge that it lacks the explanatory powers of a full-fledged theory, for example, falls into this category.

Group theory inevitably tends to reify groups and to deal with them in terms of organismic analogies. Though this problem is less pervasive in the works of the later generation of group theorists, two specific aspects of the problem are of sufficiently general relevance to deserve individual treatment. One aspect stems from group theory's emphasis on conceptualizing a group as a mass of activity and not as a collection of individuals. A group is therefore a kind of analytic or existential phenomenon. At the same time, however, the perspective of group theory demands that the group itself as the fundamental social unit pursue interests, interact with other groups, and participate in the processes of struggle that constitute a society. These two requirements create a conceptual bind from which the group theorists often escape only by treating groups as organismic entities. The second aspect of the problem arises from an economic view of group behavior based on utility theory. Returning to an interest in individual human behavior, this criticism calls into question the whole notion of an integrated group seeking to maximize some "group interest" in the struggle with other groups.[27] On the contrary, the rational individual who shares the goal of a group should be unwilling to devote his own time and resources to achieving this goal so long as it seems likely that the activities of others will achieve it for him. And if all individuals behaved in this fashion, the notion of a mass of directed activity would generally be nonsensical. This economic criticism of group theory, therefore, adds up to an assault on the utility of emphasizing groups rather than individual human beings as primary actors.

[27] This criticism is actually far too subtle to convey very clearly in a brief statement. For an interesting development of these points consult Mancur Olson, Jr., *The Logic of Collective Action* (Cambridge: Harvard University Press, 1965). Chapter I.

Group Theory

This last point raises a second broad range of criticisms of group theory that deal with the theory's anti-individualism. In one way or another all of these criticisms are reactions to the reductionism implied in the view that all, or almost all, human experience is encapsulated in the group life of a society. Several strands of this line of criticism deserve emphasis. First, many critics have expressed the view that noncategoric groups are not nearly so pervasive as the group theorists suppose, and that people (even Americans who are admittedly group-oriented) are far from being the "joiners" postulated by the theory. These critics argue that group theory consequently fails to account for many important aspects of human behavior. Second, the champions of individualism argue that the group approach fails to give an adequate accounting of a variety of social and political phenomena such as individual leadership, the sources of attitudes and opinions, or the significance of role and status considerations. The claim here is that group theory often deals with these important problems only in a definitional, rather than a substantive, sense. Third, some opponents claim that the group perspective offers an excuse to focus primarily on tangible and externally observable behavior as opposed to the more intangible influences of patterns of perception and cognition. Although Bentley's original criticism of "simple psychologism" was largely valid, new and considerably improved methods of dealing with such intangible factors are now available. Some of the later group theorists have made a number of peripheral concessions to this range of criticism. Nevertheless, group theory's fundamentally reductionist view of the individual is so much a part of the approach that it cannot be circumvented very extensively without leading to considerable confusion.

There is another range of criticisms of the group approach that are also based on charges of reductionism but that stem from a somewhat more ambiguous origin than that of the individual. The problem is that group theory is subsystem-oriented and tends to conceptualize the over-all social system as nothing more than a descriptive category by which to designate all the group interactions in a society. This conception, of course, is at variance with the concerns of a number of strands of political analysis. It leaves little room for theories concerning the public good, the common interest, or the general will. It provides only a very unsatisfactory way of treating the range of phenomena considered in analyses of political culture. The only aspect of group theory that really corresponds to the notions of political culture lies in the rather ambiguous appendage known alternatively as the rules of the game or the habit background. In addition, the approach offers very little scope for the common conception of government as a more or less unified institutional generator of interests, claims, and goals in a society. Although some group theorists have made efforts to accommodate criticisms of this sort, it is again important to point out that the fundamental perspective of group theory precludes any substantial deviation from a subsystem orientation. At this point, it is interesting to note that these two sets of charges concerning reductionism are ultimately related to the major philosophical perspectives of atomistic pluralism and idealist socialism against which the early pluralists aligned themselves.[28] This fact offers an interesting commentary on the longevity of certain very basic intellectual issues.

Two sets of criticisms that are somewhat more procedural in nature remain to be discussed. The first of these concerns the general problem of operationalization and applies in considerable measure even to the more sophisticated group analysts. The heart of the problem lies in the tendency to escape from some important conceptual difficulties by rather simple definitional procedures. If, for example, a group is not observable in terms of individual human beings, how does one discuss in meaningful terms its boundaries, organizational forms, or external tactics? The whole notion of group interests, moreover, is treated so positivistically that it is little more than a descriptive category. From this perspective groups cannot possibly have any trouble defining their interests, and it is meaningless to think of a group failing to perceive its interests correctly. Or, to take another example, how is it possible to equate the somewhat mechanistic notion of an over-all balance among groups with the mass of real world activities in many societies that often seem to bear little or no relation to each other?

Finally, there are the culture-bound aspects of the group approach alluded to earlier in this chapter. This problem seems to be a natural outgrowth of the overriding interests of many of the leading group theorists in American political processes. In short, the principal conceptions of group theory seem to be peculiarly relevant to a highly differentiated, economically modernized, and largely capitalistic social system such as the United States. A few illustrations will clarify this point. The very existence of a great multiplicity of nonprimary groups is far from characteristic of many of the world's social systems. Moreover, cross-cutting memberships resulting in a pattern of wide-ranging but rather manageable conflicts are either nonexistent or only perfunctorily existent in some systems. Or again, the implicit notions of cohesion and consensus that underlie concepts concerning extensive and influential rules of the game are presently relevant only in a limited number of social contexts. This problem of cultural limitations is not a proof that group theory is relatively useless for comparative analysis. It does, however, constitute a powerful argument for the exercise of caution in the comparative application of its concepts and categories.

[28] See pages 79–80 for a discussion of this relationship. In a wide range of disciplines this so-called "levels of analysis" problem crops up over and over again.

The
Utilization
of Approaches

The most important problem in utilizing approaches to analysis
arises from the gap between these abstract constructs
and concrete, specific research projects. Though there is an increasing
consciousness of both the existence and the potential usefulness
of the approaches, there is a widespread lack
of feeling for the techniques of moving from a general,
abstract acquaintance with an approach to its actual application
in research. This has two important consequences.
First, much of the current work in political science

manifests a sharp dichotomy between tendencies toward hyperfactualism[1] on one side and movements in the direction of excessive theorizing on the other side. And the integrative bridges are frequently few and far between. Second, there is a growing uneasiness about this problem of the gap that is leading to increased concern with these matters but that has not yet produced adequate answers to the relevant questions.

At a minimum, substantial utility attaches to self-consciousness in the selection and manipulation of approaches to analysis. In a broad sense it is quite clear that all analyses, even those that appear to be straightforward descriptions, rest on some underlying perspectives and concepts. Chapter One discusses at greater length the reasons why approaches are necessary. Though an approach may be implicit and hence unstated, it will still structure thinking and inject a variety of assumptions into concrete analyses based on its concepts and criteria of relevance. The point about consciousness, therefore, refers to the desirability of exploring the assumptions, concepts, and criteria of relevance built into one's mode of analysis, whether these be implicit or explicit.

There is also real value in conducting a mapping exercise aimed at identifying the various approaches to analysis in terms of their principal characteristics. The exercise will make the analyst aware of the dimensions of the universe of approaches. Enough approaches are now available to make it worth spelling out a list of major types. Beyond this, a mapping exercise can deal with the ways in which the various approaches relate to one another. It is useful, for example, to make distinctions both between systems theory proper and several system derivatives and among the various approaches that deal in one way or another with decisions and decision making. Finally, the construction of a map of available approaches will contribute substantially to the goal of conscious selection and utilization of an approach or combination of approaches from the list of available options.

It is impossible to bridge definitively the gap mentioned. This problem lies at the heart of political analysis and, therefore, demands continuous thought and consideration. It is, however, possible to construct certain guidelines for the utilization of approaches in concrete research. The present chapter attempts to formulate a strategy for the selection of an approach appropriate to any given piece of research. In pursuing this objective, we must first turn to a consideration of the analytic functions of approaches.

[1] On this subject consult David Easton, *The Political System* (New York: Knopf, 1953).

The Utilization of Approaches

Functions of Approaches to Analysis

Confusion abounds concerning the basic nature and functions of approaches to analysis. The wide divergences in the characterizations cited in Chapter One attest to this. And the general confusion concerning theories, models, concepts, "due process of reason," and methods in political analysis is everywhere evident. The preceding chapters, however, have set the stage for an attempt to clarify the nature and functions of approaches. Now it is important to discuss what approaches are not, as well as what they are.

A point that deserves mention at the outset stems from the fact that approaches are not full-fledged "theories" (more later on this). For this reason, judgments concerning the usefulness of an approach to analysis should be based far more on its fruitfulness than on any measure of its accuracy or validity. A reasonable correspondence with reality is important, to be sure, but beyond this the real measure of an approach is its fruitfulness in generating insights, useful questions for research, new criteria for the collection of data, and so forth. Such a posture may offend the linguistic purist worried about the influence of linguistic structures and about the uses of metaphoric or analogic reasoning, but it is necessary if approaches are to be used constructively rather than haggled over at the expense of serious applications. At the same time, it is worth recognizing explicitly that given approaches may only be fruitful for a circumscribed period of time while they are being mined by a number of analysts. There is nothing wrong with this transience if the analyst does not become too emotionally involved with any given approach.

The distinction between scope and methods in political analysis is crucial with regard to the functions of approaches. The notion of scope refers to the discussion of general areas or phenomena to be analyzed; the types of questions that should be posed in each area; and the kinds of data that might be relevant in answering various questions. Scope is, therefore, a relatively complicated subject. It includes judgments and hunches concerning values, linguistic structures, and empirical relationships. For this reason any statement proposing the scope for an analysis cannot help incorporating some influential assumptions.

Methods, on the other hand, are more nearly concerned with the tactics through which the strategy posed in a statement of scope can be carried out. Methods focus on ways in which relevant data can be acquired, placed in useful arrays, and manipulated in order to deal with the questions under analysis. Methods therefore deal with problems concerning the nature of proof and with the implementation of research tasks structured by various considerations of scope.

The Utilization of Approaches

Approaches to analysis deal, for the most part, with considerations of scope rather than with problems of method or technique. This is an important point since the failure to make this distinction lies at the heart of a good deal of the confusion concerning approaches. In general the analyst should utilize various methods in conducting research based on the same approach. Approaches do often contain elements that make them more congenial to the use of some methods rather than others. The substantive chapters of this volume contain a number of comments that address themselves to questions of this kind, but certain differences of this kind should not obscure the fact that most approaches frequently serve as frameworks for a variety of methodological operations.

It is of great importance to deal very explicitly with questions of scope especially in a period such as the present that is characterized by rapid developments in the realm of methods. Scope questions are both logically and pragmatically antecedent to the problems of methodology since they deal with the kinds of questions, hypotheses, and data to be handled by means of various methods. Moreover, setting the scope for any given piece of research is a highly important operation in its own right. Any research enterprise requires decisions that incorporate assumptions into the analysis and that provide explanations for various emphases and perspectives. These are questions of scope and they deserve to be dealt with very explicitly at the outset of a project.

Recent interest in various problems and developments in the realm of methods underlines some of the dangers of overemphasizing methods at the expense of scope. Methods are of course highly important, but their manipulation without a firm foundation in the realm of scope leads to problems. The production of quantitative data without adequate analysis of their meaning and significance is quite common. Conclusions that are thoroughly confused by the absence of solid conceptual foundations appear regularly. Many analysts fail to give adequate consideration to the difficulties and limitations of applying certain methods to specific problems in their anxiety to begin applying the methods. And methods are often applied to relatively trivial problems because of a failure to deal fully with questions of scope before the application of the methods. The tendency to value the application of methods themselves more than the problems to which they are applied is particularly deplorable; the result is a hodgepodge of confusing and unrelated streams of data. Though methods are important, it is equally important to keep them in an instrumental position vis-à-vis the strategic problems of scope and not to allow them to become masters of the whole research enterprise.

It is also appropriate at this point to discuss the place of approaches on a somewhat larger spectrum of analytic functions. Unfortunately, many

The Utilization of Approaches

discussions of these questions pose a kind of either/or dichotomy that contributes greatly to the general confusion surrounding approaches to analysis. This dichotomy contrasts full-fledged, "scientific" theories with simple sets of concepts and ordering devices.

A scientific theory is generally conceived of as a statement of variables, relationships among the variables, and predicted consequences of the interactions of the variables. The relationships and predictions are formulated deductively, but the resultant hypotheses are stated in operational terms so that they are capable of being validated or falsified through the use of accepted empirical methods. The hallmark of such theory is the existence of rigorously formulated deductive hypotheses presented in a form that makes them susceptible to inductive testing. Full-fledged theories of this kind remain largely objectives in political science since they have so far been produced in relatively few areas.

Sets of concepts and ordering devices, on the other hand, refer essentially to the topological and taxonomic work that is presently very prevalent in the realm of political analysis. Efforts along these lines are currently under heavy attack from those who are more theoretically oriented on the grounds that they do not constitute theory and that the tendency of their proponents to disguise them as theory is dysfunctional. Though it is true that the effort to create order is not a particularly significant analytic objective in its own right, work in this area is far from valueless. It does provide criteria of relevance for the collection of data, establish a basic perspective for analysis, and lend a systematic quality to work that constitutes a substantial improvement over earlier efforts.

Approaches to analysis as discussed in this volume, nevertheless, do not fit into either of these boxes. Unfortunately, discussions of the nature of approaches have often become enmeshed in the controversy over such problems as "science" and "behaviorism" in political science with the result that approaches tend to be pushed in one direction or the other. Most often, backers of various approaches attempt to push them in the direction of full-fledged theories while opponents label them mere pre-theories or sets of concepts and question whether they have any value at all.

The substantive chapters of this volume, however, should have demonstrated that in terms of functions, approaches to analysis occupy a rather solid middle ground between these two extremes. The reigning approaches in political science tend on the whole to fall closer to the conceptions associated with Snyder, *et al.*, and with Almond in Chapter One than to the more divergent views associated with Merton and Easton. The key elements of an approach, therefore, include (1) a systematic orientation and perspective for cutting into a subject area, (2) some statements concerning the central questions or types of questions that   **97**

The Utilization of Approaches

should be posed, (3) criteria of relevance for mapping out and selecting data for analysis, and (4) some guidelines for a hierarchical ordering of both questions and data in terms of significance in any given analysis.

It is possible to group the functions of approaches into several categories and to spell them out more specifically. To begin with, there are the orientational functions. It is difficult to overemphasize the importance of basic perspective. It makes a great deal of difference, for example, whether the fundamental unit of analysis is some sociopolitical system or the human individual; whether one is more interested in the results of political processes than in the processes themselves; what one takes to be a "political act," or whether one assumes political systems to be basically stable (and hence deals with their production functions) or potentially unstable (and deals with problems of system maintenance). The formulation of questions also falls into the realm of orientational functions. As mentioned previously, the language and ordering of questions tends to structure analyses considerably. Questions concerning the individual, for example, lead to very different types of analysis than those emphasizing various systems. And a tendency to give priority to questions concerning political stability will inevitably shape any consideration of political products or consequences.

A second set of functions focuses on the tasks of organization. Though order is not a virtue in itself, it is necessary to organize considerably to produce results that are understandable and capable of meaningful comparison with the outcomes of other analyses. In this sense approaches tend to spell out assumptions and to provide a systematic framework for analysis that is important in producing unified and integrated results. Moreover, though the subject is a much disputed one, it is important to mention that approaches do a useful service in providing various checklists and typologies. Checklists by themselves are unsatisfactory, but as part of an approach they aid in systematizing analysis, categorizing data, and relating variables to each other. They also contribute to a further function of approaches, facilitating combinatorial activities aimed at linking together a number of variables in as many ways as possible. Activities of this kind are crucial in breaking down rigid thought patterns.

A third set of functions centers on the production of insights. Heuristic functions based on the utilization of simplifications, analogies, metaphors, and correspondences are important results of the utilization of approaches to analysis. This is so both because approaches provide simplified models of reality and because they tend often to borrow from perspectives developed in other disciplines. Warnings about correspondence problems in borrowing and in the use of models are very much in

The Utilization of Approaches

order.[2] But it is also important to bear in mind that fruitfulness in the production of insights and understanding is a more relevant criterion in assessing the utility of approaches to analysis than some measure of sheer accuracy.

Finally, approaches encompass important recognition functions. The systematic application of various questions, combinatorial processes, and perspectives borrowed from other fields often leads to the recognition of relationships and consequences that were previously unseen; this process of recognition is one of the most important ingredients in the development of new theory in the social sciences, just as it is in the natural sciences.

Because of their antecedent nature, approaches are a prerequisite of the development of full-fledged theory. The discipline of political science encompasses many areas in which the tentative application of various approaches presently constitutes the frontier of research. In all these areas the conscious utilization of well-formulated approaches is of crucial importance. Even in areas that are somewhat more advanced, however, an openness to approaches that diverge from those that are presently dominant is highly desirable. To the extent that there are breakthroughs in research of this type, they will frequently flow from the introduction of new approaches in the analysis of subjects previously treated in terms of approaches that have been extensively mined.

Utilizing Approaches to Analysis

The principal theme of this section, as might be expected from the preceding discussion, is that the existence of a multiplicity of approaches is basically a healthy phenomenon and that the appropriate response to this situation is one that emphasizes the possiblity of fruitful coexistence among a variety of approaches. Easton catches the point well in his statement that

> each type of theoretical orientation brings to the surface a different set of problems, provides unique insights and emphases, and thereby makes it possible for alternative and even competing theories (sic) to be equally and simultaneously useful, although often for quite different purposes.[3]

Amongst the various reasons for adopting this posture, several deserve specific mention at this point. First, the discipline of political science is

[2] For some suggestive discussion consult Martin Landau, "Due Process of Inquiry," *The American Behavioral Scientist,* Vol. IX No. 2 (October 1965), pp. 4–10.
[3] David Easton, *A Framework for Political Analysis* (Englewood Cliffs, N.J.: Prentice-Hall, 1965), p. 23.

99

The Utilization of Approaches

characterized at present by a substantial lack of tidiness and order. The most basic reason for this is not the perversity of analysts working in the field; rather it is the fact that systematic analysis of most political phenomena is presently at a relatively primitive stage in which it is important to experiment freely and openly with a wide range of possible approaches and methods. In fact the energy and activity of analysts in the field at present emphasizes the intrinsic untidiness. This untidiness, however, appears to be constructive and should not be cut off in the interests of an arbitrary attempt to impose order. It is quite possible that the present confusion and haggling over alternative approaches is a temporary phase in the discipline. As time passes, it is likely that some areas of political analysis will advance beyond this stage of confusion and that order will emerge under its own impetus. If this does happen, it is also likely that much of the present haggling over approaches will subside, although the creation of a new approach will always be an important event.

The coexistence of a number of approaches is also important in light of the powerful structuring effects of language, alluded to above. In this connection the wide divergence of sources of concepts and symbolic forms manifested in present approaches to political science is no doubt healthy. Most basically, the syntax and word usages of a language structure patterns of analysis very sharply. Several analysts have pointed out, for example, that most Indo-European languages tend to emphasize cause and effect relationships for syntactical reasons.[4] And yet in philosophical terms the whole notion of causation is suspect and ambiguous at best. In addition, the dominant metaphors and conceptual perspectives of an approach are very influential in shaping analysis. The underlying differences between approaches that stem ultimately from mechanical or Newtonian perspectives and those that base themselves on evolutionary or Darwinian perspectives, for example, are very great. In fact, differences in these cases are often so great that the resultant analyses do not even belong in the same realm of discourse. These structuring effects of an approach are particularly important in the negative sense of canceling out the possibility of dealing with certain relationships and reaching certain conclusions, as compared with the more positive effects of forcing particular conclusions.

It is possible to discuss various individual approaches in terms of the tasks they are most capable of handling in the realm of political analysis. No approach is universal in the sense that it can handle successfully all the tasks generated by the requirements of political analysis. It is therefore important to make specific inquiries concerning the task performance of any given approach. Approaches differ substantially in terms of subject

[4] See Harold and Margaret Sprout, *The Ecological Perspective on Human Affairs* (Princeton, N.J.: Princeton University Press, 1965), pp. 45–46.

The Utilization of Approaches

areas in the general field of politics to which they address themselves. Upon inspection, it turns out that most of the important approaches have been constructed with a built-in thrust toward one or two of the broad, subject area categories distinguished in Chapter One. These divergences in the orientation of the conceptual material of approaches stem from the differing perceptions and perspectives of their creators, and it is important to take them into account in discussing the task performance of any given approach. A second distinction focuses on the types of questions that characterize any given approach to analysis. Approaches tend to generate certain patterns of basic and orienting questions that, to a large extent, typify the approach and form the basis of any analysis utilizing the approach. In addition it is often possible to distinguish approaches in terms of the analytic operations that they are set up to handle most easily and that they tend to encourage by their structure or organization. There are, for example, several approaches that appear to be particularly congenial for comparative analyses; others have a built-in orientation toward the generation of correlations, whereas still others tend to structure thinking in the direction of causal statements. This distinction concerning analytic operations should not be overemphasized, but it is a factor worth considering.

It should therefore be possible to discuss the performance of any given approach in handling specific tasks. In many cases it will be possible to make reasonable judgments of such questions on the basis of simple techniques of inspection. In other cases the utilization of specific indexes of performance should be explored. Examples of indexes of this kind include (1) richness and comprehensiveness of resultant descriptions, (2) fruitfulness in generating hypotheses, (3) combinatorial capacity, (4) usefulness in uncovering previously unthought-of relationships, and (5) suggestiveness in selecting models for more detailed analysis. These indexes stem from the various functions discussed in the preceding section, and it would be possible to vary them to emphasize particular functions of interest.

It is probable that attempts to develop composite utility measures for the various approaches would be rather meaningless and misleading. And there is no strong need to pose questions of this over-all nature concerning approaches to analysis. Since approaches overlap in performing certain tasks, however, it may well be possible to apply indexes of the type mentioned above on a somewhat more specific basis. This leads to the possibility of developing some reasonably solid grounds for selecting among the various approaches when it comes to particular parts of a given research project.

This leads to a strategy for utilizing approaches to analysis that is based on a kind of "constructive eclecticism." It is important here to distinguish several types of eclecticism. The present discussion does not   **101** advocate the kind of eclecticism that would result in an amalgamated approach based on borrowing elements from several of the available approaches. Nor does it lead only to a posture of emphasizing the elements of value in all approaches and letting it go at that. Though these forms of eclecticism are quite common, they are ultimately not particularly constructive.

By way of contrast, the strategy advanced here centers on the proposition that research should progress from the subject area to be analyzed to the selection of an approach, rather than from a commitment to an approach to the selection of substantive research topics. All too often, loyalties to a particular approach lead to a somewhat undiscriminating search for areas to which the approach in question can be applied. An antecedant awareness of the alternative types of approach is, in fact, important. In setting up a particular project, however, it is most important to consider first the subject area one desires to treat and the kinds of questions for which answers would be most useful. At this point it is important to range through the available approaches considering their comparative utility in dealing with the questions that have been posed. There is no eclecticism here in terms of subject areas for analysis. The eclecticism comes in abandoning loyalties to a given approach in favor of a flexibility in matching approaches to substantive questions for analysis.

From this perspective it is also quite possible to consider utilizing material from several approaches in the same piece of research. Different approaches may be applied to various subsets of relevant questions, or they may be applied to the same substantive areas in the hope of producing either corroborative results or substantially different slants on the same subject. In mixing approaches in this fashion, there are some important potential pitfalls to be kept in mind; these deal with (1) confusion of approaches in analyzing results, (2) incommensurabilities in cases where the results of applying different approaches are to be compared, and (3) the continuing problem of correspondences between the relationships suggested by an approach and the relationships existing in real phenomena. Such problems are particularly salient when approaches are mixed, but they are almost always avoidable and should not be taken as prohibitive limitations on a research strategy involving a mixing of approaches.

The Utilization of Approaches

A further source of confusion surrounding approaches to analysis lies in the theological context in which they exist.[5] The result is, in effect, a world of competing sects without any dominant group or accepted orthodoxy. Followers of the various approaches tend to acquire emotional commitments and loyalties as contrasted with an intellectual flexibility that would view all the approaches as potentially useful tools. The result is a tendency to pursue unmixed doctrines and to preserve them unsullied against the intrusions of adulterating forces. Needless to say, this theological posture poses a major obstacle to the form of eclecticism outlined above.

The general theology of approaches breaks down into several categories. To begin with, there are some questions concerning the genesis and propagation of approaches. They tend to originate in a true process of creation. Most of the approaches stem ultimately from the work of one individual or, at most, a rather small and finite group. The creator tends to be moved by a perceived lack of utility in using the reigning approaches and he is generally willing to reach out to other areas of political science or to other fields for the essential ideas, concepts, and metaphors underlying a new approach. Moreover, most of the existing approaches have been set forth in the form of a kind of abstract framework rather than promulgated in the course of a series of substantive studies.

Of considerable importance are the phenomenon of discipleship and the relations between disciples and creators. Time and again the creators of major approaches to analysis gather a group of disciples around them in the course of their work in a rather peculiar relationship. It is functional for the creator not so much because he needs people to spread the doctrine as because he needs people to apply his superstructure. The large-scale approaches constitute very extensive frameworks that cannot ultimately be judged until analysts have applied them to a variety of substantive problems. The creators, however, are generally incapable of performing this task both in terms of temporal resources and in terms of basic temperament. The disciple relationship, therefore, becomes important. For the disciple, the relationship is at best ambivalent. He often gains certain short-term advantages because the creators tend to wield considerable power in the academic world and can see that their disciples acquire positions of various sorts. This is sometimes a short route to the acquisition

[5] I have deliberately couched the following comments in very strong terms. In this form, they are not of course *fully* applicable in many cases. A sharp statement of these issues should, however, clarify the problems and emphasize the important difficulties in question.

103

of a foothold in academia for young scholars. Nevertheless, discipleship in this realm, just as in any other context, tends to be limiting and intellectually stultifying in the long run. The relationship often attracts individuals who are not notable for their imagination or originality. And the relationship itself forces the disciple into the role of implementer or executor of the creator's ideas. Over time, the result of this structured relationship is likely to be very substantial frustration or a movement toward the role of defender of the faith and of doctrinal purity. In both cases the result is generally unproductive in terms of the interests of the discipline as a whole.

Another focus of the theology of approaches concerns the phenomenon of *doctrine*. Though the doctrine of the creator is often new and imaginative, it tends to be transformed rapidly, in the hands of his interpreters, into dogma and into the tenets of a new orthodoxy. Unfortunately, in the process the approach often loses the qualities of imaginativeness and flexibility that made it attractive as an alternative to the previously reigning approaches. The development of a new orthodoxy is also closely associated with the problems of heresy and heretical movements. In a theological environment attempts to question elements of an approach and to suggest alternative formulations threaten to undermine emotional commitments and are therefore branded as heresy. In the realm of approaches to political analysis, the fight against heresies is frequently instigated by the disciples who are inevitably less secure in their faith than the creator himself. The defense of orthodoxy, however, frequently draws in the creator since he has a vested interest in the activities of his disciples and since his talents are often required to defend the approach against criticisms. Defending an approach against criticisms generally results in the production of additional dogma of an exegetic nature. And whereas the original conceptions may have displayed a certain economy of formulation, the new dogma is almost inevitably more elaborate and involved since it stems from a variety of efforts to explain and defend the approach in the face of widely diverging criticisms.

The facts that there is no *dominant* sect at this time and that the competition among sects is rather sharp place additional stress on various problems of defending the faith. Although a period in which one sect is securely dominant may be conducive to relaxation and at least peripheral innovation, the present period in which several important contenders are active is one of rather sharply-drawn conflict. In this light the phenomenon of puritanism has become important. Puritanism emphasizes the clear-cut nature of the boundaries between camps or sects and limits the amount of divergence that is possible without approaching heresy. In addition it tends to reduce tolerance by emphasizing a dichotomous view that forces indi-

The Utilization of Approaches

viduals to take a position clearly for or against any given approach. The phenomenon of puritanism in political analysis is further complicated at present because it exists in respect to methods as well as to scope. In the realm of methods, camps divide, for example, between behavioral or quantitative techniques and more "traditional" techniques. Puritanism in regard to scope is a very different phenomenon, though it occasionally tends to correlate or overlap with the development of methodological camps.

There is no doubt that approaches to analysis are necessary and that they can play a constructive role in political analysis when applied in a thoughtful fashion. The tendency for approaches to acquire the trappings of theology, however, is highly dysfunctional from the point of view of advancing the discipline of political science. It is important to be clear on the major dangers and pitfalls involved.

To begin with, there is a real sense in which an approach can become a theological prison. Imprisonment in the trappings of an approach frequently undermines the creativity of even the best minds. There are several distinguishable elements in this process of imprisonment. Earlier discussions have stressed the tendency of all approaches to structure thought in important ways. Structuring of this kind becomes highly dysfunctional when the analyst insists on loyalty to a single approach for all purposes and especially when he utilizes it over a long enough period of time for the structuring effects to become ingrown. The result is a kind of "blinders effect" that resists innovation. Related to this are the inhibiting effects of a sense of commitment to and defensiveness concerning a given approach. Loyalty of this kind emphasizes the blinders effect and often leads to the expenditure of energy on exegetic rather than substantive work. A further difficulty stems from the common inflexibility of the committed. Whereas flexibility in utilizing approaches is the hallmark of the eclectic strategy outlined earlier, commitment to the orthodoxy of a single approach tends to reduce the analyst's freedom to follow such a strategy. Finally, the problems of reification are frequent by-products of commitment to the utilization of a single approach. Whether the reification involves systems, groups, or communication networks, it is a source of confusion that is exacerbated by a theological posture concerning approaches to analysis.

There are also some special problems arising from the insistent orthodoxy of disciples and more distant followers who spread the doctrine of a given approach. The creators of approaches, who usually possess creative and innovative minds to begin with, frequently display a certain agility and tactical flexibility in manipulating their own approaches. As is often the case in theological environments, however, the disciples and

The Utilization of Approaches

followers commonly lack this agility and are prone to be more orthodox and doctrinaire than the creator. They are able to attain the security that the creator attains through a sense of creative command only by rigidly applying the rules and regulations prescribed by the approach. This situation only accentuates the problems of imprisonment outlined above; also it sometimes reduces the contribution of the creator by forcing him to support and defend the productions of his followers.

A further dysfunction of a theological posture from the point of view of advancing the discipline centers on the problem of wastage. As mentioned above, analysts committed to a given approach tend to expend a great deal of time and energy on exegetic contributions to the controversy among sects rather than on substantive analysis. The one thing that might ultimately demonstrate the worth of an approach in a clear-cut fashion—successful applications to a variety of substantive problems—tends often to be left out in the process. The emotional rewards of conducting the competition among approaches are therefore frequently purchased at the expense of intellectual progress.

All this adds up to a situation characterized by a significant lack of constructive bridges linking the various reigning approaches or sects. There are two main sources of this phenomenon. The theological thrust toward doctrinal purity creates an atmosphere in which there is little interest in exploring the connections among approaches, let alone techniques for harnessing them in tandem. At the same time the emotional requirements of loyalty and the tendency to brand innovative pressures as heretical push the approaches farther apart than they are in any objective sense. Efforts are more often directed toward underlining differences, therefore, than toward building bridges.

For these reasons, a posture that emphasizes the existence of various middle grounds is frequently a somewhat uncomfortable one. Those who assume such positions are often ostracized and attacked by all sides, which means that they tend to become isolated in a way that reduces their influence. All this is not to argue that there is any intrinsic virtue in assuming a middle stance; many suggestions for compromise are practically worthless. As regards approaches to analysis, this tends to be the case when the middle ground consists of a bastardized approach based on straightforward borrowings from a number of existing approaches. Yet in political analysis the middle ground, when properly defined, seems to offer far more promise than a theological posture in support of any given approach. The relevant middle ground consists of a research strategy that gives priority to substantive problems (rather than to loyalty to an individual approach) and emphasizes the eclectic selection of an approach or mixture of approaches on the basis of the needs of a given piece of research.

The Utilization of Approaches

To Explore Further . . .

Being on the whole a rather self-conscious and introspective lot, political scientists have written extensively in the area of self-analysis. Though much of the resulting work is either peripheral to the concerns of the present volume or highly confusing, there are a number of works that deserve exploration. Amongst those of a more general nature, one should consult Robert Dahl, *Modern Political Analysis* (Englewood Cliffs, N.J.: Prentice-Hall, 1963); David Easton, *The Political System* (New York: Knopf, 1953); Vernon Van Dyke, *Political Science: A Philosophical Analysis* (Stanford, Calif.: Stanford University Press, 1960); and Roland Young (ed.), *Approaches to the Study of Politics* (Evanston, Ill.: Northwestern University Press, 1958). There are, of course, many additional works that deal with specific aspects of the problem of approaches to analysis. Amongst these, the following seem especially suggestive: Gabriel Almond and James S. Coleman (eds.), *The Politics of the Developing Areas* (Princeton, N.J.: Princeton University Press, 1960)—Chapter One of this book is especially important; David Easton (ed.), *Varieties of Political Theory* (Englewood Cliffs, N.J.: Prentice-Hall, 1966); Carl Friedrich, *Man and His Government* (New York: McGraw-Hill, 1963); and Martin Landau, "Due Process of Inquiry," *The American Behavioral Scientist*, Vol. IX, No. 2 (October 1965), pp. 4–10.

On the problems of general systems theory several sources deserve mention. The most important single source is *General Systems*, the yearbook of the Society for the Advancement of General Systems Research, which has been appearing annually since 1956. Another basic source is the symposium volume emanating from the Chicago meetings of the 1950's: Roy R. Grinker (ed.), *Toward a Unified Theory of Human Behavior* (New York: Basic Books, 1956). Beyond this one should turn to such works as Norbert Wiener, *The Human Use of Human Beings* (Garden City, N.Y.: Doubleday, 1954); Talcott Parsons, "An Outline of the Social System," in T. Parsons, E. Shils, K. Naegele, and J. Pitts (eds.), *Theories of Society* (New York: The Free Press of Glencoe, 1961), pp. 30–79; and James G. Miller, *Living Systems* (forthcoming).

Structural-functional analysis has evoked a very considerable debate in recent years. For the conceptions of early proponents consult: B. Malinowski, *A Scientific Theory of Culture and Other Essays* (Chapel Hill: University of North Carolina Press, 1944), and A. R. Radcliffe-Brown, *Structure and Function in Primitive Society* (London: Cohen and West, 1952). For later formulations and applications see, *inter alia*, S. F. Nadel, *Theory of Social Structure* (London: Cohen and West, 1957), and Samuel Beer and Adam Ulam (eds.), *Patterns of Government*, 2nd. ed. (New York: Random House, 1962). Perhaps the single most well-known critique of structural functionalism is Kingsley Davis, "The Myth of Functional Analysis in Sociology and Anthropology," *American Sociological Review*, Vol. 24, No. 6 (December

1959), pp. 757–772. There exists, unfortunately, no significant writing dealing with the kind of input-output approach to politics elaborated by David Easton.

On the general perspectives underlying approaches stemming from communications theory and cybernetics consult Colin Cherry, *On Human Communication* (New York: Wiley, 1961), and Norbert Wiener, *Cybernetics,* 2nd ed., (Cambridge, Mass.: MIT, 1961). Interesting examples of efforts on the part of political scientists to utilize these perspectives appear in Richard Meier, *A Communications Theory of Urban Growth* (Cambridge, Mass.: MIT Press, 1962) and Philip Jacob and James V. Toscano (eds.), *The Integration of Political Communities* (Philadelphia: Lippincott, 1964). The leading, albeit opposing, conceptions of decision making are set forth in David Braybrooke and Charles E. Lindblom, *A Strategy of Decision* (New York: The Free Press of Glencoe, 1963), and Herbert Simon, *Administrative Behavior,* 2nd. ed. (New York: Macmillan, 1957).

Harold Lasswell is both the originator of the distributive approach to political analysis and the dominant figure associated with the approach. Additional books of his that are relevant to an understanding of the approach include *Power and Personality* (New York: Norton, 1948), and *The Future of Political Science* (New York: Atherton, 1963). Far and away the most impressive effort to utilize and apply a distributive approach to analysis stems from the activities of the group interested in "law, science and policy" at the Yale Law School. Lasswell himself has been very much involved in this project, but the most important guiding figure is Myres McDougal. To date the project has produced several large volumes as follows: Myres McDougal and associates, *Studies in World Public Order* (New Haven: Yale University Press, 1960); Myres McDougal and Florentino Feliciano, *Law and Minimum World Public Order* (New Haven: Yale University Press, 1961); Myres McDougal and William Burke, *The Public Order of the Oceans* (New Haven: Yale University Press, 1962); and Myres McDougal, H. D. Lasswell, and Ivan Vlasic, *Law and Public Order in Space* (New Haven: Yale University Press, 1963).

There is a relatively large literature that falls under the general heading of group theory. For further elaborations of the original conception see Arthur F. Bentley, *Relativity in Man and Society* (New York: Putnam, 1926). A particularly interesting and well-known effort to pin down some of the group bases of American politics in a detailed fashion is V. O. Key, Jr., *Politics, Parties, and Pressure Groups,* 5th. ed. (New York: Crowell, 1964). For various analyses and critiques of group theory consult, *inter alia,* Richard W. Taylor, "Arthur F. Bentley's Political Science," *Western Political Quarterly,* Vol. V, No. 2 (June 1952), pp. 214–230; R. E. Dowling, "Pressure Group Theory: Its Methodological Range," *American Political Science Review,* Vol. LIV, No. 4 (December 1960), pp. 944–954; Myron Q. Hale, "The Cosmology of Arthur F. Bentley," *American Political Science Review,* Vol. LIV, No. 4 (December 1960), pp. 955–961; Robert T. Golembiewski, "The Group Basis of Politics," *American Political Science Review,* Vol. LIV, No. 4 (December 1960), pp. 962–972; and Harry Eckstein and David Apter (eds.), *Comparative Politics: A Reader* (New York: The Free Press of Glencoe, 1963). Perhaps the single best-known critique of group theory appears in Stanley Rothman, "Systematic Political Theory," *American Political Science Review,* Vol. LIV, No. 1 (March 1960), pp. 15–33.

To Explore Further

Glossary

Boundary (or *boundary condition*): A line, area, or statistical measure that separates two completely distinguishable classes of things thereby serving as a determinant of inclusion and exclusion.

Closed system: An isolated system having no significant interaction with an environment.

Equifinality: The quality of reaching the same final state regardless of divergences in initial conditions or processes of change.

Equilibrium: A state of rest brought about by the interaction of opposing but balancing forces.

Homeostasis: Dynamic self-regulation; the ability of a system to maintain its fundamental, internal balances even while undergoing various processes of change.

Homology: Structural similarity or correspondence between system components.

Learning capacity: The ability to engage in processes of self-modification in response to (usually repeated) external stimuli.

Negative entropy: The tendency to move toward relationships of increasing order and organizational complexity.

Open system: A system that interacts with an environment (1) in the sense of receiving inputs and producing outputs, and (2) in the sense of adapting internal structures and processes to the environment.

Operationalization: The specification of measurable empirical referents for abstract definitions, concepts, and hypotheses.

Organismic system: A system that either is an organism or can be meaningfully treated as an organism where the chief qualities of an organism are (1) relatively fixed ordering of components, (2) reproduction of the same type or species, and (3) existence of a life cycle.

Overload: Quantitative or qualitative demands on the capacities of a system or communications network which it is incapable of handling in the time allotted.

Positive entropy: Tendency for the components of a system to seek their most probable distribution, i.e. randomness or maximum disorder. (This is often called the Second Law of Thermodynamics.)

Reification: Treatment of an analytic or abstract relationship as though it were a concrete entity.

Security dilemma: A competition for security (arising from suspicion or mistrust) among two or more actors or social entities that proves self-defeating due to the unobtainable nature of absolute security.

Stability: The tendency of the variables or components of a system to remain within defined and recognizable limits despite the impact of disturbances.

Starvation: Reduction or stoppage of the flow of quantitative or qualitative inputs into a system that are necessary for its continued functioning (starvation is the opposite of overload).

State-determined system: A system whose path and/or final state are uniquely determined by the initial state of the system regardless of the way in which the initial state came into being.

System levels: Hierarchical ranks for systems in terms of (1) geographical scope, (2) inclusiveness of membership, (3) range of functions, or (4) relationships of authority.

Ultrastability: The ability to modify internal relationships and/or to influence environmental conditions in the interests of neutralizing actual or potential obstacles to the maintenance of stability.

Glossary

Index

Frames of reference: analytic tool, 9–10
Function: analytic unit, 4; definition, 29–30
Gain: in negative feedback, 53
Gatekeeping function: input-output theory, 40–41
General systems theory: attitudes toward, 19; change concept, 18, 22; core concepts, 17–18; critique, 24–26; descriptive concepts, 18, 21; empirical analysis, 22; isomorphism and interlocking systems, 16–17, 22, 24–25; limitations, 23–24; origins, 14; pattern maintenance, 21–22; system definition, 15–16; transfer aid, 22–23
Geography: unit of analysis, 2
Goal attainment: analytic concept, 7; group theory concept, 89; input-output theory concept, 45; Lasswell's concept, 74; negative feedback process, 58–59
Goals: Deutschian concept, 52–55, 58; group theory concept, 89; Lasswell's concept, 75; Snyder's concept, 64
Government (see also Politics): group theory view, 84–87
Green, Thomas Hill, 80n
Group theory: change concept, 89; critique, 90–92; descriptive powers, 88; goal attainment, 89; group layers, 83; group relations, 82–83; history, 79–80; human group concept, 81–87; influence tactics, 83; interest concept, 81–82; internal organization, 83; nature, 87–88; pattern maintenance, 88; patterns of control, 88–89; political role, 83–87
Hagan, Charles B., 81n
Homeostasis: defined, 54; Deutschian approach, 54
Ideology: distributive analysis theory, 69; structural-functional theory, 36–37
Incrementalism, 62–63
Index stability: defined, 71
Individual: analytic unit, 3–4, 98; group theory approach, 86, 90–91; Lasswell's approach, 68–69, 71, 74

Influence: analytic variable, 6–7; Lasswell's theory, 66–69, 74; Snyder's theory, 64
Information retrieval, 5
Inputs: demands, 39–41, 43; support, 41–42
Input-output theory: analytic system, 37–38; change concept, 44–45, 47–48; core variables, 38–39; critique, 46–48; decision concept, 42; demand variable, 39–43; environment concept, 38–44; feedback, 43–44; goal attainment, 45; membership system, 37–38; patterns of control, 45; politics, 45–48; power and influence concepts, 45; support variable, 41–42; systems use, 37
Institution: analytic unit, 2, 4
Interest: group theory concept, 81–82
Interlocking systems, 16–17
Isomorphism: general systems theory, 16–17, 22, 24–25
Kaplan, Abraham, 66n, 70n
Kardiner, Abram, 35n
Lag: in negative feedback, 53
Landau, Martin, 99n
Language (see also Symbols): interpersonal communication, 11; political analysis, 100
Lasswell, Harold L., 61n, 65ff
Latham, Earl, 82n, 84, 86
Lead: in negative feedback, 53
Learning (see also Feedback): decision process, 58; goal-changing feedback, 55–56
Legitimacy: Lasswell's approach, 70
Levy, Jr., Marion, 28–29, 31–33, 35n–36n
Lindblom, Charles E., 62n, 63
Load: concept defined, 52–53
Load capacity: defined, 52
Locke, John, 80n
Macroanalysis, 23
Malinowski, Bronislaw, 28
McClosky, Herbert, 64n
Membership: analytic concept, 6; Easton's concept, 37–38
Memory: Deutschian theory, 51
Merriam, Charles, 73n
Merton, Robert, 8, 20, 29–30, 35–36, 97
Method: defined, 95
Microanalysis, 23

Mill, John Stuart, 80n
Models: Deutschian approach, 50–51, 59, 61
Naegele, Kaspar, 3n
Olson, Jr., Mancur, 90n
Open system, 21–22
Orthodoxy: in political analysis, 103–106
Outputs: authority decisions, 42; feedback loops, 43–44
Overload: concept of, 18
Parapolitical system, 38
Parsons, Talcott, 3n
Pattern maintenance (see also Equilibrium; Stability): analytic concept, 6; Deutschian approach, 54–55, 57–58; distributive analysis approach, 73–74; general systems theory approach, 21–22; group theory approach, 88; structural-functional approach, 34
Perception: approach function, 10; input-output theory, 43; Snyder's theory, 63
Pitts, Jesse, 3n
Policy-making: analytic unit, 3–4, 7; general systems theory, 24
Political science: systematic analysis and, 100
Politics (see also Government; Ideology): "broad" and "narrow" views, 4–5; group theory concept, 83–87; input-output theory concept, 45–48; Lasswell's concept, 66
Power: analytic unit, 2, 4, 6; Deutschian approach, 57; general systems theory, 24; Lasswell's definition, 66–69, 74; Snyder's schema, 64; structural-functional theory, 34
Practices: value distribution, 69
Purposes (see Goals)
Radcliffe-Brown, Alfred Reginald, 28
Random aggregate, 15–16
Ranney, Austin, 3n
Recall: defined, 52
Reception systems (see also Feedback): Deutschian concept, 51–52
Recognition: analytic function, 99
Revolution (see Breakdown; Change)
Robson, William A., 2

Rodee, C. C., 2
Russett, Bruce, 61n
Sapin, Burton, 9–10, 62n, 64n
Scope: analytic variable, 6; defined, 95–96; Lasswell's definition, 67
Shils, Edward, 3n
Simon, Herbert, 63n
Snyder, Richard, 9–10, 62–64, 97
Society for the Advancement of General Systems Research, 15
Sprout, Harold, 100n
Sprout, Margaret, 100n
Stability (see also Pattern maintenance): analytic concept, 6; Deutschian concept, 54–55, 57; general systems theory concept, 18, 20–22; group theory concept, 4; Lasswell's concept, 74
Starvation crisis, 22
Stress (see also Demands; Dysfunction): general systems theory, 18; input-output theory, 38–42, 47

Structural-functional analysis: change concept, 32, 34; critique, 33–37; function distinctions, 29–30, 32–33; general systems theory links, 28; goal attainment, 34; history, 28; pattern maintenance, 34; patterns of control, 34; requisite alternatives, 31–32; static nature, 32, 36; structures, defined, 30
Structure: analytic unit, 4; defined, 30
Subjectivity: in analytic approaches, 11–12
Support (see Inputs)
Symbols (see also Language): distributive analysis theory, 69
System: analytic unit limitations, 24; definitions, 15–16; Deutschian decision-making, 50–56; general systems theory, 25; input-output theory, 37–38; isomorphism and interlocking systems, 16–17; structural-functional theory, 28–35

Time: input-output theory, 40; system definitions, 15–16
Transfer (see Communications)
Trend analysis: distributive analysis theory, 71–72, 75
Truman, David, 81n–83n, 84–85
Units of analysis: approach alternatives, 8–12; "broad" and "narrow" views, 4–5; decision process, 3, 50ff; geographic, 2; human group, 81–92; individual, 3, 68–69, 74; institution, 2; Lasswell's view, 66; policy-making, 3, 7; power, 2
Values, 51; distributive analysis theory, 65–69, 74–75
Van Dyke, Vernon, 3n
Violence: distributive analysis theory, 69–70
Von Bertalanffy, Ludwig, 14
Weber, Max, 2
Weight: analytic variable, 6; Lasswell's definition, 67
Young, O. R., 21n